AN INDIAN ODYSSEY

An Indian Odyssey

PAT BUCKLEY

Also by Pat Buckley

Down Under Roundabout and Up There

Published by
Kirriemuir Publishing

Also available from amazon.co.uk

Copyright © Pat Buckley 2005

First published in 2005 by
Kirriemuir Publishing
25 West Cliff
Preston PR1 8HX

British Library Cataloguing-in-Publication data

A catalogue record for this book is available from the British Library

ISBN 0-9546406-0-9

Printed and bound by Alden Press, Oxford

Contents

Acknowledgements

My thanks go to Dipti and Barry for inviting me to India, her mother, father and brother for being gracious hosts, my friends Cath Holliday, as proofreader, Julia McManus, for endless encouragement and belief in the project and to Chris Johns, Sue Baumann, Joy Crosbie, and all the others for their friendship and support.

And finally, to my family, for every time I've said, 'Sorry, I'm doing the book' and being so very understanding. Again many thanks and much love.

Foreword

Pat Buckley was widowed at fifty and since then has travelled, usually alone, but always independently. She relates her travels in letters to friends and family and from these she has adapted them into a book. This was her first experience of third world travel in 2000, but since then has visited sixteen more countries, many of which are retold in her first book, Down Under, Roundabout and Up There. She has made every attempt to be accurate within the limits of her memory and her knowledge at the time of writing.

This book is for anyone who sits at an airport, relaxes on a beach, reads in the bath or never gets beyond two chapters before succumbing to sleep. It is inspirational, hilarious, informative and totally relaxing.

CHAPTER ONE

Backpacking via the four star hotels

For me, buying a 21 day "Discover India" ticket on Indian Airlines was like giving an open bottle of whisky to an alcoholic.   I just couldn't resist.

The whole of India lay before me. Not just Rajasthan and Bombay but the south and even the Himalayas, as it slowly percolated through just what I could do. This was to be my gap year, rather late, but as they say, better than never.

I definitely felt as I approached the Himalayas by jeep like a backpacker – albeit one who was backpacking via the four star hotels. Camping had never been my thing, I didn't know a toggle from a woggle, a tent-peg from a guy-rope. Hostels and I had never even been on nodding terms. I'd passed by them but never thought of entering. Something to do with being brought up with, "If it's not the best, don't do it, go there or attend it." Better to stay at home than put up with inferior accommodation.

I've no doubt my mother's attitude made sure I missed out on some great, spontaneous, cheaper holidays, but as it was so deeply ingrained in me from an early age, I wasn't likely to be changing now, which is why it is backpacking via the four star hotels or nothing.

You know, I'd never wanted to go to India. The poverty, the heat, the smells, the creepy crawlies, the list could stretch forever. It hadn't been mystically calling me over the years. It was something I'd avoided. I always shuddered when someone said they were going. My mother must have given me more Freudian hang-ups than my convent education, although I don't know, it's probably fairly evenly divided between them.

So, why was I going? I, a determined and independent woman, was about to embark on a journey that was to change the way I thought of myself and life in general.

Well you see, I was asked. As simple as that. My Indian friend, Dipti, who performed a myriad of tasks to make the Buckley body conform to recognized ideals of beauty, asked me.

She was just finishing waxing, polishing and buffing me with my pre-holiday massage, and was excitedly telling me about her forthcoming six week trip to India. Just as she tweaked my big toe, she said, rather casually, "Why don't you come to India, Pat, you'd love it?"

There was a pause and she said, "You know you can come." — middle toe.

The funny thing was I did know I could go.

So by the time she'd reached my little toe, — I was going.

Now I don't hang around re: decision-making but this surprised even me. About ten seconds was all it took. To visit a country which filled me with horror, fascination and foreboding.   Ten whole seconds. There'd been many more places high on my must-visit list ahead of India, in fact nearly everywhere else on the globe. Yet I had a horrified fascination with the challenge it presented. Perhaps life doesn't get any better than this.

As Dipti left I gave her the cheque for the air fare – £460.00. Barry, (short for Bharat) her husband, picked her up and on hearing of our plans looked panic-struck. Did I know what I was letting myself in for? It wasn't like England – I'd have been very disappointed if it had been – it was dirty, very dirty and the water – everything was different and not in a nice way. I know it's different, and it was the very difference that was attractive. I felt exhilarated, the excitement of doing something so spontaneous, so impulsive had set my pulses racing. Is this what life in the fast lane's like? I . . . was going to India.

At first I thought he might not want me to go with them but it turned out he was worried his birth country would not suit me. Once he realized I knew it wasn't like Britain and would not have too high an expectation, he was rather pleased.

They were already booked, Barry, Dipti, Benita and Priscilla. After much uncertainty they were able to get me on the same flight. I gave them the money and they arranged my visa via an uncle in Leicester.

I found, as with most Indians, they like to do business with other Indians and the travel agent was, of course, one too.

It was then the warnings began. I would have to be careful, there were many, many cheeky Indians. I would not be allowed out alone. Even they would be escorted everywhere as they would be recognized as European Indians. The very cheeky Indians, we all had to beware.

What sort of a country was it where even native born Indians weren't allowed to wander alone? By the end of September I'd know.

CHAPTER TWO

Howling winds,
horizontal rain, fate

Actually my journey to India in September 2000 started in the Spring of 1999. The local college had a reflexology course and I'd been ringing to see when they were taking clients, i.e. guinea pigs.

You don't expect to travel to India on a life-changing experience just because you braved the howling wind and horizontal rain of a bitter March night as you tramped across the vast car park of the local sixth form college. You have to be keen to be out on a night such as this, huddled in your coat, collar up, running to the warmth of the heating and the bright lights

The reason I was doing this was because normal rates for the treatment were fifteen pounds. So, to save the princely sum of nine pounds I was willing to subject myself to the rigours of a winter's night. I just can't resist a bargain. Somewhere in the mists of time I think I've got Scottish or Yorkshire ancestry lurking in the background. I'm probably not a really fully-fledged Lancastrian at all.

Unbeknownst to myself or Dipti, fate was already deciding that within two minutes of my leaving the car park my first steps to India would be taken. I would forge links which would affect both our futures. Mine would never be the same again.

On reaching the beauty department I was shown to an alcove. There, a shy, young Indian girl worked away at my nether regions. She said that she was going to go mobile when her training was complete. She would be charging the same as the college. I was hooked.

Over the next eighteen months we built up a friendship, I met her two girls, then her husband, we exchanged Christmas gifts and in many ways I became a mother figure to her, as her family were in Gujarat.

As is usual whenever I have the opportunity for a grand tour I am always just going to North Wales. In this case, Dipti had come to give me my beauty treatment to last me for the next month before I returned.

So there I was, trying to get a map of India, difficult, and a Lonely Planet guide, easier, (wrong age, wrong attitude, but who cares?) in Porth Madog. I devoured the guide, fell on it like a starving woman. Suddenly India was THE place to go.

We were leaving for India at the end of September as the monsoons finished. The idea behind this was that, in theory, it should be cooler – if only.

Originally I'd told Dipti I would go for 3 weeks, but rang the next day to say 4 weeks. Barry thought that was a good idea, because he said by the time I'd adjusted to the food and water and got over my tummy bug, one week would have gone. One week in the loo did not sound good, but this was all part of the experience. You can't make an omelette without breaking eggs etc.

CHAPTER THREE

Oh ye of little faith

My eldest son, an inveterate traveller, warned me to make sure I'd put weight on before I went as everyone he knew lost at least a stone when visiting India. I gently pointed out to him that, flattered as I was, didn't he notice I had a stone to lose? Where had he been looking all these years? I know parents are sometimes invisible to their children but I'd never though of him as unobservant.

The same son had given me a lightweight travel bag to contain all major documents, monies, credit cards etc. It had about fifteen zippered compartments. Oh joy. Although I'm a seasoned traveller, I was a bit green when it came to this bag. In the same way you wear "in" a new pair of shoes, I hadn't worn "in" my bag. By the end of the trip I'd know exactly what was in each compartment, but arriving at Bombay airport at 11.30pm, I was clueless. Confused and clueless is a fairly good description. Thank goodness I didn't know what was in store for me as I landed or I might have stayed on board.

So armed with my jabs and malarial pills I left on September 28th. The family in India were thrilled Dipti was bringing a friend and were looking forward to being my host. I had tried to do my bit with a trip to Waterstones for a Gujarati dictionary. Apparently one wasn't printed. So I asked Dipti if she had one. It duly arrived. On opening it I found hieroglyphics and that was how I ended up on Indian soil knowing just please and thank you!

We set off up the M6 in a minibus. There were the five of us and some friends of Dipti going on a European holiday, so nine in all. The warnings kept coming thick and fast about cheeky Indians. Then suddenly I was not allowed out alone because it was very dangerous. We'd gone from cheeky to dangerous. Cheeky sounds cute, dangerous sounds, well, dangerous – unpleasant, violent, to be avoided. So far, I'd understood that they only might swindle me out of my worldly goods, and my honour would be safe. But now it was dangerous? I was under threat and I was still on British soil.

Too late to turn back now, I was on the M6 in a minibus heading to Manchester airport in the company of eight Indians who seem to think my chances of survival in their home country was zilch. Oh ye of little faith.

At the airport more warnings as we waited for departure. I could see they were quite worried about me. In the meantime I wondered what I'd let myself in for.

I'd mentioned that I wanted to go to Rajasthan, bells began ringing – I couldn't go alone – I would need an escort – I felt like I was entering Beirut at the height of Hezbollah.

By now I was feeling quite excited as I didn't know what to expect. I'd never done third world before. I kept trying to imagine Bombay (or Mumbai as it's now called) at midnight. How exotic would it be?

One of Andy, my son's, friends had said that at Bombay railway station the rats were running over his feet. I never found out if this was as he stood on the platform awaiting his train or slept on the platform, as he was a backpacker. He also said they'd been in some of his hotel rooms, along with other exotic fauna of the area, namely cockroaches. But, as we know, thanks to the upbringing delivered by my mother, there was not much chance of my occupying a room of a similar type, unless, of course disaster struck. And how was I to know that on more than one occasion during the next few weeks that disaster was imminent?

CHAPTER FOUR

Indian fox hunting

I'd been seated separately from the family on the plane and was jammed in the middle of a row, I didn't rush to leave. I was nearly the last off and due to the heat on board I'd taken off my silk linen jacket and put it with my hand baggage in the lockers at the end of the row. As I stood waiting to exit the row, I couldn't see the jacket, just my bags. Realization dawned, as I saw an Indian woman just leaving down the aisle with a familiar looking item over her arm and I was still stuck in the row of seats. Desperation made me call, "Excuse me, is that your jacket?" Her reply was to hand my jacket back to me across two rows of seats as though nothing had happened. I was amazed. Not a flicker of guilt, sheepishness or embarrassment. She just kept walking.

Anyway it wouldn't have fit over her M & S large ladies' cardigan. She probably meant it as a present for one of her family. Thank goodness the matching trousers were still on my body, if she'd got the set that it would have been a major coup for her. Everything Dipti and Barry said was true and I hadn't even left the plane and they were trying to fleece me. How on earth would I survive once I'd left the "safety" of the plane?

This incident threw me and from then on I was very wary. But do you know something, not once in the next six weeks did anyone try to steal from me again! That was a one-off but it unnerved me and it's only on looking back that I realize that basically the Indian people are not thieves. Some will swindle the arse off you, face to face, but I think they feel they've given you a sporting chance if they can see the whites of your eyes. A bit like their version of fox hunting.

Anyway back to the plane. Hot, bothered, the air-conditioning was now off, I made my way to the exit. Many people were staying on as the next stop was Bangkok. As I emerged with a growing sense of dread, I expected to see Barry, Dipti and the two girls at the entrance. No-one. I looked back on board, couldn't see them. I headed off down the tunnel to arrivals.

As I approached the immigration hall, it struck me that I hadn't got my do-it-all, go anywhere handbag. I frantically searched. Nothing. I'd have to leave my bags with the family and return to the plane.

There were seething masses in various queues as I stood at the top of the steps but I couldn't see them. How could I miss a family of four? I shouted for them at the top of my voice, many faces turned to look at the panic-struck, red-faced, perspiring Englishwoman, but no one admitted to knowing her and who could blame them?

Sheer panic overwhelmed me as I raced back to the plane dragging my hand baggage, getting heavier by the minute. A rather warm Brit presented herself at the aircraft's door just as a flight attendant was leaving with my bag over her shoulder. At the same time, Barry and Dipti appeared through the same door. Had Christmas arrived all at once? One of the girls had felt ill and they'd been in the toilets till then.

My bag had dropped off as I struggled through First Class. I now felt that my trip would be plagued from start to finish and if it wasn't cheeky Indians, it would be all my own doing

So there I was drained and I'd been on Indian soil

for approximately 15 minutes. Things could only get better – but not yet.

Siege mentality had taken over. But once I'd been properly re-united with the family I tried to be the nonchalant English woman again. Taking deep breaths as I emerged once more into the immigration hall, I hoped no-one recognized me as the perspiring, incoherent, wild-eyed woman of earlier.

I took my place in the queue with the family where we waited for nearly two hours. The officials are painfully slow, relishing their power (however briefly) over our lives. Remember we taught them all about bureaucracy and they seem to have been eager pupils. In fact I think we could learn lessons from them now. They've made it into an art form. Time means nothing, speed is something a train or a car does. Deliberation, cogitation, consultation, form-filling, Tony Blair or any bureaucratic apparatchik would be thrilled to see it exercised at such a high level. Even Labour and all its red tape would be an apprentice in India.

Surprisingly enough it was Dipti who, with two girls still feeling sick and the humidity stifling, complained in a high voice that it was disgraceful to keep us waiting this long with two young children. Something must be done. And amazingly something was done.

One of the officials looked up and they were dealt with next, with me getting by on their coat tails. I was so relieved. I don't do heat, it does me. I am not at my most lucid, composed or attractive in heat.   Grief, I sound like one of my son's dogs.

We came through baggage and customs without a hitch and reached the arrivals hall just before one o'clock.

We hit the velvet night and to my relief no rats were running over my feet, no hawkers were trying to bamboozle me out of my clothes, money or goods.

Dipti's family had come to meet us. We were greeted with the traditional garlands, mainly marigolds, and a bunch of flowers each.

Her mother, father, brother and uncle were there. Only her brother spoke halting English. I was still rather shell-shocked, not only had I nearly lost a jacket but through my own fault I'd nearly lost everything to get me into the country. The bag had just slipped off my shoulder. I now had it bandolero style across my body and that's how I travelled for the next six weeks. I may make mistakes – but I am a quick learner.

Magic hands took our luggage and I'm glad to say the next time I saw it it was in my bedroom. We then went to get our liquor licence. Yes, that's right, our liquor licence. For someone who could live teetotal if I had to, I was puzzled.

It was explained to me that Gujarat, where we were heading, was a dry state and if you were travelling in a car which was stopped by police and you had drink in it you would be arrested if you didn't have a licence.

That was good enough for me. Anything to keep me out of an Indian jail in this heat. So far I'd not had a good start. Jacket, bag, would prison round it off nicely?

We trailed round for around half an hour whilst the staff played pass the parcel with us – but eventually we arrived at the correct desk to receive our three free permits – We were on our way.

First we dropped off the uncle where the family had stayed the previous night in the suburbs and then headed for the main road to Ahmadabad. Little did I know what lay in store.

CHAPTER FIVE

We need a convoy

I lost my fear of India during the most traumatic road trip I have ever made. I decided if I didn't die on this road, then I wasn't meant to and would be ok for the rest of the trip. My time had not yet come. It made me feel I was invincible. Sometimes terrified – but always invincible. Whitewater rafting would hold no fear for me, after all remember, it wasn't my time.

You get a certain fatalistic feeling when you are not driving and therefore cannot influence the outcome. I knew we had five hours before we arrived at Valsad. This was the main road for everyone, including thousands of trucks, between Bombay and Ahmadabad

I have rechristened it the road to Hell but I think I'm being generous there. Despite what I had been told it was 8 hours of sheer horror throughout the night. I twitched between torment and terror.

I could see the headlines in the newspapers now, "British tourist killed, injured, spirited away, whilst travelling in a hired minibus en route to Gujarat. Some Indians were also killed. The pot hole swallowed the minibus whole, but it must be emphasized this only occurred because it was avoiding the pot hole on the other side which could have swallowed an entire HGV." Talk about devil and deep blue sea.

The road was so pitted that although it was only one lane each way, much of the travelling was done on the wrong side because the holes were better. Whilst I was still with it at the start of the journey I watched what was happening. This freaked me out so much I decided ignorance was bliss. I ducked my head down behind the seat in front and pretended it wasn't happening.

Indicators are not used on most Asian roads, just the horns. We weaved in and out and as we returned to our side we were missing oncoming HGV's by the odd centimetre. I am not exaggerating. No-one gave way, you thought that that was it many times, but the skin-of-our-teeth springs to mind.

The side of the road (this is THE main highway, often only two lines wide) you travelled on was dictated by 4 things; the size of the pot hole on the other side; the blind corner (always overtake, use only horns); how many HGV's are coming towards you – they must be at least two abreast – and finally if your horn alerts the guy in front (normally HGV), that you will need room to squeeze in, in 2 seconds.

They seem to think that blaring the horn confers a charmed life on them, no-one would dare crash into them head on, after all, they had pommed. I know how people must have felt travelling hundreds of miles by stagecoach. Jarred, battered and shattered.

About 45 minutes after we set off we stopped at a service station. I use this term loosely. Loosely because it depended upon what type of service you wanted. If it were tyres changed, repaired etc, there were many. If it were brakes, brake linings, you could take your choice. In fact it looked like you could have your car/van rebuilt, and all on offer 24 hours a day.

Now if you wanted loos, well this is where it gets a bit iffy. I followed the others because I thought I should. There were many flies, cockroaches and you could smell it long before you got there. It was the usual hole in the ground, with foot places on either side. Nothing surprising there, since it's not too many years since a brasserie on the Champs Elysees was still sporting this time-honoured system of ablutions. For all I know it could still be there.

But despite having this wonder of the 19th century in situ, it still smelt like most of the men preferred to use the side of the hillside overlooking the main road as a quick means of relief.

I bought a bottle of water at a kiosk and made my way back to the bus. The air was still warm and of course there was an abundance of mossies. I'd no spray on and wondered if my malarial pills would work. I was new to this third world lark.

We hung around for a bit and it would have been nice to start off again. Inquiries revealed that we were waiting for some more vehicles. It was safer if we could go in convoy. I thought it best not to ask why it was safer as I might not have liked the answer.

Eventually we were off again. Fortunately as the night wore on I became so exhausted and resigned to my fate that I began dozing on and off, waking with a jerk every so often to look at my watch and ask Dipti how much longer. After five hours she then started hedging by saying just a bit longer. I gave up in the end. I just presumed I was there forever like being on the London Circle Line, but with bumps and jarring thrown in. It was an endurance test. I'm sure my, "Are we nearly there yet?" had come from somewhere deep in my childhood psyche. I just hoped it didn't sound as plaintive as my children used to sound.

Just eight hours after leaving Bombay, 24 hours after leaving home, we drew up at my new home. As we turned into the street off one of the main roads through Valsad, the street's own family of goats wandered up and down, 3 or 4 cows and calves, a few dogs, unclaimed, 3 pigs, black and pot bellied, some hens and some chicks. The donkeys would appear later. Welcome home Noah.

CHAPTER SIX

Temple by the shore

So now I've found out there's Indian time and English time, if an Indian says 5 hours, allow 8. The minibus parked up opposite a ground floor garage complex. Eight stiff-legged travellers exited. We made our way towards the lifts. The garage was big with enough room for about 30 cars. I presume one for every apartment in the block. It was open plan, just like a small municipal car park underneath a shopping centre.

The apartment was on the third floor. As I was being looked after, I didn't have to worry about baggage, all this just appeared by magic in my bedroom. As is normal in Asian communities, everyone took their shoes off at the door and left them on the marble floors of the corridor. Each apartment had a concertina iron grill door with a big padlock for when the premises were unoccupied. Further to this, by way of security, most families I visited had a grey, metal, double wardrobe, which was also locked with a big padlock. This was where they kept their cash and valuables, and I would say most Indians seem to keep a fair amount of cash at home.

Despite all these stringent precautions I never saw or heard of thefts or robberies. Perhaps it was just cautiousness on their behalf.

As we entered the apartment I was prepared for what it would look like. Dipti had said it had marble tiled floors and walls. Other than the look of luxury this created, I suppose this was cooling as well. It was very spacious, the main room was narrowish, about 11 ft wide but very long, about 20 ft. At one end to the left was a verandah with a garden swing in the middle and it had wooden bench seats on either side along the wall. They were a bit like an old-fashioned settle.

To the right as we entered was a door leading to a double bedroom with a European loo and shower en-suite. The other door out of this bedroom led to another verandah. This was used for putting out the washing and also had plants in it.

Halfway along the living room opposite where we'd entered an archway led to a short corridor and facing you in this was an Indian toilet and then a shower room. On one side of this was the kitchen and on the other side another double bedroom. This was to be my room, whole and entire. Just for me.

We went to bed at 8.30am as we arrived. My guilt at occupying 50% of the sleeping space had not had time to rear its head yet. There was a fan above the bed and its settings were from one to six. It usually ran on six when I was conscious and four when I was sleeping. I put my Evian spray for cooling my face and body by the bed, my water bottle was just beside that and I settled down to recoup my energies.

We all reappeared about teatime. We had a drink, food was being prepared and we sat around chatting. Dipti's parents could not speak much English. Her father, now retired, had forgotten most of what he knew, her mother was picking up words. Due to my lack of success in obtaining a Gujarati dictionary, my linguistic skills were even worse.

After eating and leaving more than they thought I should, it was proposed that we went to the temple, Dipti's favourite, by the sea. Did I want to go? Well of course I didn't want to miss anything. I wanted to experience it all – well I'm sure I did.

Once outside the heat was oppressive and draining, but the minibus was air-conditioned. It wasn't due to be returned until the next day.

We arrived at the beach after about 15 minutes drive. Darkness was just beginning to fall, which it did variably depending where I was in India between 6.00 and 6.30pm.

You could hear the surf crashing in as we entered the temple. Just Dipti and I went in. The girls followed. We sat on the marble floor and Dipti went up to the shrine. Out of the Hindu Gods, Dipti worships Sai Baba, a male God. There was a life-size statue of him at the front of the shrine.

As we sat there I could see small ants, the sort we have in England, dashing about the floor. It looked like the worshippers were a great inconvenience to them. Serious detours were required. This was the same temple Dipti's parents came to pray when she was seriously ill just lately. They spent hours every day making offerings and praying.

Dipti had taken flowers to offer and shortly after she did this, all the women, and there were quite a lot even though it was a small temple, had to leave. Dipti explained that as it was a man-God and his robes were changed for the evening, women were not allowed to remain. There were 3 or 4 men who re-arranged all the flowers and offerings as people placed them and it was their job to change the garments. Also another thing I found unusual and almost quaint was the fact that women could not attend the temple whilst menstruating. I've since found out that many religions ban women during this time. I do know in many African tribes women were sent outside the village as they were considered unclean then. It makes me feel Christianity is extremely enlightened on this issue. Also Dipti cannot wear a gold medallion of her God then. She told me as well that after eating meat they have to bathe before visiting the temple.

We left the temple in the dark, I could still hear the surf but couldn't make out the sea. We entered the beach and there were still stalls selling fruit and drinks. I was offered a coconut, freshly cut, and as I said yes, a straw was placed in it.

Now this was my first drink after all the dire warnings about checking the source etc and I wondered if the straw were a new one, a second hand or one even older, this being a common trick. Coupled with this was the fact that coconut, normally, made me feel violently ill. I sipped apprehensively, the flavour was refreshing, let's face it, any drink was refreshing in that heat. The liquid did not have the "coconut" flavour which makes me heave. I have since found out that this is the only part of the coconut I can take, and generally speaking it's uncontaminated.

I've seen it done many times since on the holiday programmes, but this was only Autumn 2000 and watching a young boy with his machete slice the top from the coconut and trim it was still a novelty.

We returned to the apartment and I retired to bed, still not knowing I was using 50% of the sleeping room. Various aunts and uncles appeared to be visiting as well, but I thought they could live round the corner. It was only after a day or two I realized they were all sleeping in the same apartment.

It was as I went to use the European loo in the middle of the night and I came out from the little corridor into the living room. I had to pick my way across mattresses arranged across the floor, as far as the eye could see. Later on, in the visit, when I saw how it was done, each family slept on a double mattress. The spare mattresses were kept under the bed in Dipti's room. The bed folded back to reveal the mattresses stacked underneath – about half a dozen of them.

This was not normally done in front of me as I was the official visitor and like all of us we don't always let our visitors know what's going on behind the scenes. The swing on the verandah was one bed, the benches on either side, two more. Dipti, Barry and the girls had the other bedroom.

Usually Sanjay, Dipti's brother, his wife Ranee, who had given birth to her second child three weeks earlier, and their daughter, Dani, had that bedroom. I was using mum and dad's, and they used a mattress. So when they returned after I'd been there two days Sanjay and his family had another mattress.

Because Dipti, Barry and the girls had not visited for 5 years, people were coming from all over the province to visit them. Due to the difficult travel conditions they, by necessity, needed to stay for a few days. I would think that that was recovery time after the road to hell. So some nights perhaps over 20 people were sleeping in the apartment. It makes the sleepovers at the Buckleys (so many children often stayed my family had regular fire drills) seem like small potatoes. Our maximum was usually 12.

CHAPTER SEVEN

There's THEM and there's us

The next morning I managed to rise by 10.00am. I appeared to have got over any jet-lag. As I'd been drifting out of sleep before rising I could hear so many different noises and I knew someone had come into my room. Sometimes mum came in to get something out of the wardrobe, but most mornings a woman in her early twenties crept in and swept the room with a special broom which was made of curved soft twigs. She swept under the bed and very quietly disappeared again.

When Ranee returned with her two children after the first two days, every morning before I rose I could hear the baby crying. An Ayah came in and massaged the baby, surprisingly the baby cried when this happened. Serious crying. Indians also use head massage on babies with colic which I know works wonders.

So my morning dreams were interrupted by so many different noises and eventually they began to have a soothing effect on me. It also meant I was doing everyone a favour by not appearing before 10.00am. They could get all the chores of the day out of the way before their guest needed attention.

As soon as I got up breakfast appeared. So my second day there, after a leisurely breakfast, was a shopping trip to downtown Valsad. Dipti's father took us to the end of the road and began negotiations with a ricksta driver. There was enough room for Dipti, her mother and I, the haggling went on for only about thirty seconds. This was a quick deal. I only realized later we could have been stupendously ripped off for 10p if we'd not negotiated.

At this time I had not used Tuk-tuks or similar, but the Indian version is a far smaller affair. Two, possibly 3 people and a piece of luggage can fit in. It's really like a motor bike with a cab on top. Very rickety, called a ricksta by the locals.

I was mildly excited as we set off. This was third world hands-on. The breeze was cooling, it needed to be. After about seven minutes we arrived. Downtown had the look of a bazaar, a very busy bazaar. There was a guard outside the gold jewellery shop, which seemed to be packed with customers. Gold jewellery is much esteemed by Indians and can make up quite a large part of a dowry. There was a guard inside too. We would shop there on the last day for me to take presents home.

This visit was to buy shoes and clothes of course. The shoe shop was narrow, about 20ft long, allowing for the shoes stacked on each side, floor to ceiling – I think the shop was the store room – the space in between the walls was no more than 3ft. The owner was there and he had three young Indian lads rushing – yes in the 3ft space, – up and down. Once we'd sat down on the bench, they'd about 18" to work in. Sweat was pouring off them. Then again, it was pouring off me, but this time, being a woman, mine was only perspiration.

The amount of energy they used to sell me two pairs of shoes, £7.00 in total would have run a small village for two days. The sale was everything.

Next on the list was a dress shop. As a visitor I was always placed on a chair under a fan. I had the ubiquitous water bottle with me but still wondered if I would have to be carried out when it all got too much.

There was a dress, loose-fitting which I liked and it needed trying on. Must I?

Now this is where the revelation occurred. To try this on I had to go upstairs. As I did I passed all these women queuing on the stairs which were stifling. I went past them and through the door at the top into another world. A world of ice-cold air-conditioning, a rarified atmosphere. This was the MEN'S DEPART-MENT. Not for them the whirring of hit and miss fans, not for them the free-for-all of women and children wilting as they waited if a spare fan couldn't be found for them to sit under.

This was the THEM and US. Briefly I was one of THEM, but this was quickly dispelled when I entered the changing room. Cramped with boxes it was small but I suppose adequate. As I slipped the dress over my head I felt something tangled in my hands. When the dress dropped down I could see above me a conglomer-ation of electrical wires and I was happily playing amongst them. They disappeared into the roof and walls at various levels, but had a look of a Thomas Salter electricity kit which had been given by mistake to a seven year old who was never going to be the next Thomas Edison. The wires were doing loop-the-loop between my fingers and I was deeply worried I might do the unforgivable and disconnect the air-conditioning.

I escaped back onto the shop floor and went down to purchase my dress. As I reached the top step, the heat was appalling and the women were still there with their children waiting for their menfolk. Don't think feminism stands a chance there.

Back home and mum began making the evening meal. I was not expected to do anything and to be perfectly honest I feel that existing in that heat is the most they could ask of me. Everyone sat on the kitchen floor eating. Only I ate at the table. Sometimes Barry joined me, I think to make me feel more at home. I would have sat with the others on the floor but the mess I made even with a formal setting meant I would have disgraced myself further.

My laundry was taken away and came back the next day, washed, ironed and folded. I still felt guilty. It was the young girl who swept the floors who did the washing in the shower near my room. One side was sloping so that washing could be beaten and then rinsed under the shower. Mum did the ironing. I tried to explain, nothing I had needed ironing. It was against my religion. I don't even think Dipti could translate that.

Most of the time it was a mix of talking to Dipti, Barry and the girls and reading and doing crosswords or puzzles whilst I let the family get on with catching up. After all five years was a long time. I didn't want them to feel they always had to include me. I tried to be a "good visitor." Afterwards Dipti said her parents had enjoyed having me as I was an easy visitor. I hadn't been demanding over food and went along with all suggestions for doing things.

Well that was the impression I wanted to create as my hosts had generously looked after all my needs and put up with a visitor in their house during their beloved daughter's visit. We all know how straining it can be to have a stranger in your midst for a long period of time. A short period is sometimes too long.

Once mum realized which Indian foods I preferred she started making milder curries and some of the vegetables had only a slight tang. No matter how long I stayed I could never manage more than 3 chapattis and never any rice. Most of my food came in small dishes which I never really managed to finish, and I ate, as is the custom, with my fingers. I was in a mess, but I was doing it. The table had a look of a child of about twelve months old still mastering its spoon. I usually cleaned up after myself. That was one thing I really felt obliged to do. Something to do with shame I think. It was the way the food fell out of the chapatti on the way to my mouth.

I offered to share my big double bed with one of the girls, but they just left me in it, I now slept at the wrong end because that was where the fan was over my face. Extreme conditions require extreme measures.

I was fussed over all the time and kept getting new dishes to try. When it seemed I couldn't take the heat any longer, Dipti, myself and the children, went fifty yards to the end of the road and there was a most wondrous thing. We crossed the road, passed the guard (in a very hot uniform) seated on his chair and entered my lifesaver. It was called Happiness and that was exactly what it was. We would sit on the verandah and order fresh-pressed juices, mango, pomegranate, pineapple, custard apple and nearly anything else you could name and they arrived ice-cold in minutes. One day I took the children and bought two bars of Cadbury chocolate, 3 Kit-kats and four fresh juices for the magnificent sum of £2.20.

When I went into another juice bar downtown, the temperature was not quite cold on the fresh fruit juice which now raised the question, were they putting ice cubes in at Happiness and if they did, where were they getting the water?

I kept waiting for the Delhi belly but it never arrived. Just the odd bit of stomach ache which was understandable given the different food I was eating. Allowing I'd not had tummy trouble the idea of my losing weight whilst I was there was fading fast. I'd probably be the only person to visit India and put on weight. Mamma, mum or Mrs Bulsara (yes same surname as Freddy Mercury) as she was known to some, seemed to think I needed feeding up. She must be wearing the wrong glasses. My feet and ankles were now swollen, but I was resigned to that.

I had adjusted to the heat most of the time, but at the beginning I must have looked like a red blob, a big wet, red blob with a bottle of water.

I shall never believe Dipti again. She said to bring a jacket for when it is cold in the evening. The night of the garage dance – all will be revealed – it was 85° at midnight with 70% humidity.

As I'd been warned by Barry that India was a dirty country I was surprised how clean, though grubby and dusty it was. I'd expected sheer filth, so I had been reasonably impressed. It cannot be easy keeping things clean in the heat and dust. Damage limitation I would imagine is the most you can do.

So damage limitation with me meant switch the fan up to number six as I appeared and fetch a fresh bottle of water. How alarming did I look? Pictures of me taken at the beginning look dire, but the longer I was there the more normal I looked. There had been talk of a woman who kept a peacock in the apartment block opposite. I was curious.

The roaming animals on the streets were like street entertainment laid on by a circus. There was the odd camel wandering around, cows naturally had the run of the place and just ambled along the side of the road eating where they wished.

But really the animals there are amazing, they were

all so laid back, calm, serene, as if they know they're Indian. They seemed to have more road sense than most UK citizens. None of them ever darted about near traffic. They appeared to make rational decisions and move steadily and calmly in their chosen direction. And this is all the animals I've mentioned plus a few cats. The one exception being the cow sitting quietly chewing its cud in the third lane of a ring road in Bombay. Our ricksta managed to miss it. It's like old McDonald's farm. Other than cows, goats and dogs appeared to have the streets sewn up. The dogs were sleek and mongrel type, a bit like a fat whippet. You rarely saw a dog by itself. There was usually a crowd of them and they walked purposefully as though they were on a mission and believe me if they were around the meat market at night they could be dangerous. I think they think we would come between them and the leftovers. We are a rival and therefore we're a legitimate target. One of my Indian students became hysterical when she saw one, single, friendly dog, in the UK. It was awhile before she calmed down.

Most of the cows in Valsad sit on the central reservation when not wandering. Every animal, cows, pigs, goats, dogs, chicks, donkeys feed themselves from the refuse on the side of the road. India is not the tidiest country, I don't think they have landfill sites. They don't need them – they are recycling as only the Indians know how.

During all my time in India I never saw any animal faeces on the streets and I've walked around a few, stepped over all sorts, but not that. The other thing I never saw sight or sound of either was mice or rats. Both the above surprised me. They must be somewhere, perhaps it's Bombay main station.

CHAPTER EIGHT

Bruised knuckles and egos

Just down from Happiness on the next block a building was having renovations. Renovations was probably a bit grand for what was happening, but the scaffolding would have UK Health and Safety reaching for the smelling salts. It consisted of long tree branches about 10 inch diameter or less which were fastened together with pieces of cloth or wires. I think it was whatever came to hand. Flimsy seemed too robust a word to describe the structure. It was the sort of thing, though the shorter version, we in the UK would use to train our clematis up. We'd probably feel that a heavy-duty ivy might cause the whole structure to collapse and wouldn't risk it. I took pictures because I couldn't believe my eyes. That said, no-one seemed to come to any harm as they worked 25ft up the structure, which might make you think Health & Safety in our country has gone too far for far too long.

Dipti informed me that we were going out that night. It was a dance. As this was the build up to Diwali, it was like the UK with its parties etc around Christmas time. The dance in question was a competition to find the best dancers in the region. 5,000 would attend.

So I was got up in my skirt (bought that day) my own top, a silk sash across my body and I was given a Binda (the teardrop-shaped marking on the forehead) to wear – they come in handy stick-on types – some jewellery I'd bought in town and I was duly launched on Valsad society.

Dipti had bought a beautiful sari that afternoon, so dolled up to the nines, glistening quietly in the heat we set off.

Set off is not quite all we did. The general mode of transport there was motorbike or scooter, so Sanjay (Dipti's 30 year old brother, father of the new baby) and his friend drove both of us on their bikes, which meant my having to negotiate my way including very full skirt onto the back of Sanjay's bike. Being a westerner and not realizing I should sit side-saddle I got on astride the same as I had when I was seventeen, which, I'm ashamed to say, resulted in the bike rearing up at the front like a hell's angel impressing his latest bitch on their first outing. I fell backwards but Sanjay quickly recovered and we were off. Flying through the night as others whizzed by on their bikes, all the female passengers riding side- saddle but for big, white mama who didn't know the form.

First we paid a visit to Hemman (one of Dipti's best friends) and his wife and family. She had got a little street party of her own going and about eight of us danced around in a circle. Before we left mum had taken me on one side and showed me the rudiments of a dance and they were suitably pleased with me. In the privacy of the living room I was Wayne Sleep. It was to be a different matter at "The Dance."

I felt a bit self-conscious at Hemman's dancing on the dirt road as Barry camcorded this for posterity. I only got it wrong now and again. Barry and the girls had arrived by ricksta. Since Dipti teaches dance at the temple in Preston, the girls were experts. The only amateur was the Preston clog-dancer.

Soon Dipti wanted to go to the big one. Barry and the girls were despatched home and we set off (all of us side-saddle this time) to the dance. Our scarves, sashes, saris flying in the wind, zooming in and out of traffic, avoiding pot holes of course. No matter how bad the roads I travelled over the next six weeks, nothing would ever compete with the road to hell. After that, everything was in perspective.

The dance was held in a big enclosure, open air, with refreshments inside at the entrance. As we paid and walked towards the "dance floor" a giant cockroach ambled, not scurried, away across our path. I think it was overdosed on Coca-Cola and orange juice, this being a dry state, only non-alcoholic drinks were on offer.

You could hear the noise as you approached. It was in the round with a large stage to the left. On it a band, consisting of one singer and about twelve other players who were giving it all they had. The centre was covered with thousands of people in the most exotic dress, whirling, a bit like dervishes, one way and then the next. Everyone was in unison. They could have formed a five thousand strong formation team and taken all before them.

Children as young as six or seven were managing as well as the older ones, which, looking back, were about thirty years old, tops. I'm surprised I ever thought I was eligible to join, but not wanting to be an awkward guest and also wanting to experience everything, we plunged in as the next dance started.

Now, unfortunately it was a stick dance. This was the one mum had been teaching me, but without sticks and I'd only had to concentrate for about sixty seconds before I was declared competent.

This time I was given two 12 inch sticks, on the

lines of drumsticks. I watched Dipti. Now they always say so long as you do your best that's all that matters. I feel there are some people in Valsad the next day who would say that that's no excuse.

Anyway it didn't put one young Indian off as he tried to pick me up – not literally – just in the "do you come here often" vein. They'd let him out especially for the dance I think, and his crayons were in his top pocket. You see, they presume I'm younger than I am because people of my age in India are over the hill and they certainly don't do the stick dance in public.

As it was a nationwide competition I could see TV camera crews here and there. I have found out that an Indian song and dance doesn't finish for about thirty minutes. If it's good enough for one chorus, it's good enough for fifty, and I would be quite willing to bet that in about thirty years time the whole Indian nation will be deaf, as the noise level makes you almost feel sick.

Sanjay and his friend just watched, it was as if this were Dipti's treat because there's nothing like this for her in the UK. For the stick dance, it was danced in two giant circles which went in different directions, a bit like a progressive barn dance – now where did that come from? My childhood somewhere – so naturally you met a different person every minute or so, which was how it came that a large minority of the inner circle were nursing minor injuries the next morning, courtesy of the English clog dancer.

I thought I'd got the hang of it, the rhythm was flowing, then I came upon someone who instead of two sticks and one click, gave one stick, one click, another stick, one click. It wasn't quite pandemonium amongst the ranks, but I have to admit confusion reigned in my little corner of the world.

I'd been doing so well and here I was out of sync. It was quite a few damaged knuckles later before I recovered my co-ordination, and then along came another clever clogs with the same devilish combo and I was off again. Frank Spencer was better co-ordinated than I was. Eventually the ordeal of the young and fit of Valsad and surrounding areas was over. I was going home. Sanjay had been holding my bottled water and I drank greedily. Mounted the bike with considerable aplomb – I couldn't stick dance – but I was now an experienced sari biker.

We arrived home to greetings of how it had all gone. Dipti duly reported I'd done well only to have this refuted by something which could not lie the very next day. At 11.00 am just after breakfast the next door neighbour came in and announced that the English visitor was on TV. Heavens above, I'd only been there forty eight hours. They turned on the TV and there was the dance and me. The cameras were there to film the top bands and the top dancers in the country and they were filming me. Now I'm not saying I won, but as we know, there were a lot of bruised knuckles and they weren't mine.

Everyone was very excited and Barry said, – oh please don't let it come true – that I might be very lucky and it be shown on Indian TV in Britain as this was an important dance. It was bad enough knowing how badly I'd done without most of the Indian sub continent and all their British counterparts knowing about it.

CHAPTER NINE

Four doors down from McDonalds

It seemed to be the Indian custom to keep your main door open all day so any of your friends or neighbours could just wander in. One must presume because of this then that Indians normally only indulge in playful activity during the sleeping hours. It was very much a close community and as in Britain in "the old days" everyone helped everyone else. The next door neighbour, she of the TV star info, brought specially-prepared biscuits for the English guest. Their son was still only four and his hair was very long and tied on top of his head from where it flowed down. It was explained to me he would only get his hair cut when he was five. It was a rule of his religion and the branch they followed demanded this. His elder sister was about nine and spoke excellent English. She was at an English medium school and was given the job of escorting me to Happiness one day when I said I was going. I HAD NOT to go alone. It was dangerous. How it was dangerous was not satisfactorily explained to me, but this mystery could be solved by the presence of a wisp of a girl of nine, who was blessed with a firm grasp of English. On our safe return, Dipti said we'd go one day to see the woman with a peacock in her apartment.

The next afternoon it was time for a foray to Daman. Valsad is almost on the edge of Gujarat which means they can easily visit Daman in the next province to buy their liquor. After about one hour's drive we arrived at what looked like an off licence paradise. Row after row of shops selling drink. We were travelling with Hemman, who had a car, Barry, Dipti, her father and me on this important trip. Dipti's father had a motorbike, as had Sanjay , so Hemman having a car was a bonus. Hemman was well-off by Indian standards. He owned a gold jewellery wholesalers. It would think it was a licence to print money.

So this trip was the reason I'd to have my liquor licence in case I was caught in a car without said licence and I was carted off to non-air-conditioned pokey. The mind boggles. Bet there's no Euro loos there.

I bought some bottles of spirits to give to Dipti's family, which coupled with the presents I had already got them, didn't seem enough for the superb hospitality I was receiving.

As we left Daman we went to an hotel for drinks and I had a good look round the area as I'd just been told I'd be coming there when the family went to a temple eight hours drive up the mountains for Dipti to complete her vow to her God. I didn't demur as the thought of another eight hour drive – as they'd admitted it, it could be twelve hours – was as welcome as a hole in the head.

That evening mum took us to a restaurant – vegetarian food – just me, Dipti's family and her. The main dishes were only 60p each. More than you could eat. Puddings are rarely eaten, but mum once made kheer for me and it was exquisite. I've had it since but it wasn't as good as hers. Fresh fruit is often eaten and with the abundance they have I'm not surprised.

Dipti was very popular at home. People, especially young ones, kept arriving from all over to see her and she held court with supreme confidence. What a change to see her there compared to England. In India her assurance is complete, in England she's a bit diffident, wanting to do the right thing and not always sure if she is doing so. I have seen the longer she stays in the UK that she is growing in self-assurance, but in India she is the pop princess, top of the heap, Miss Personality.

It was announced that we were going to Bombay the next day on the train. Barry, Dipti, Sanjay, Hemman, his wife and I. I was pleased at this as I had already told Dipti I would *never* travel the road to hell again, I was finished with it. It had had one chance with me and it had used up all my nine lives and some of my ancestors' as well. It could even have used some of my next door neighbour's as well.

And so we took a ricksta to the station and Sanjay negotiated. He managed to get three first class air-conditioned and three second class non air-conditioned. Well there wasn't much of a debate as we three women deposited ourselves in the first class. It was to be between three and a half and four hours to Bombay – I'd passed the toilets on the way to the seat and vowed come hell or high water I would never need them. And I have to say now in the four further trips I took my vow was never broken, to my great relief.

I was full of trepidation as I entered the station. I'd been moderately protected – hell, they'd put a fortress round me and here I was exposing myself to dangers – as I say, whatever danger had never been phrased – and I stuck close to the rest. It wouldn't have been so bad if I'd known what I was looking out for.

In Bombay, among the beggars we encountered at

the traffic lights were unusually tall women. Very striking and so different that you just know that they're men. Sanjay said they were outcasts as they were hermaphrodite and this was the only way to earn money.

Quite a few possibilities had been mooted for staying the two nights in Bombay. Most of them had no air conditioning as part of the bargain price. Hostels were mentioned and I now asserted myself in the interest of self-preservation, tip no. 43.

At this stage of my life I had never lived in close proximity to so many people for so long and not been in charge of the situation. This was my escape and like many children when first away from home, homesickness takes over, in my case independent luxury was rearing its head. I got out my Amex Platinum Hotel Book and saw deals in Juhu Beach at Holiday Inn. It had air-conditioning, swimming pool – oh please let it be cool – restaurant and all the other goodies, boutiques, cool lobbies, chandeliers.

The others didn't want to spend that sort of money, which I can understand. Eventually Hemman stopped the taxi at a place with quite a few hotels. I didn't know where we were but they had said earlier that Juhu was a long way.

I went in to an Indian-run hotel and it was gloomy and the air-conditioning was smelly and noisy. It was half the price of one of the chain hotels, which in turn was less than the Holiday Inn. It was still tremendously hot and trailing round hotels was losing its appeal.

I said I would pay for us to stay in the the chain hotel – 3 women in one room, 3 men in another. Hemman gave me something for the one night they spent with us, but I realized I couldn't ask the rest to pay for the luxury when it was at my insistence. I just wanted the freedom to swim, and chill out on my own.

That night the others were going to a dance in downtown Bombay. So long as I didn't have to leave the splendour of my air-conditioned hotel, I was happy.

I got on the phone to Caroline, one of my daughters, and she warned me it would be costing a fortune, well it did – £76.00. But I needed that. I'd enjoyed my four days in India so far, but I needed to talk to one of my own. Just really about how different it was.

Caroline also told me that the Saturday I left, one of my student houses (At this time I still had some houses for students at the university) had had a window smashed and she had to get out an emergency glazier. So within hours of my leaving the meltdown had started. Now it's a strange thing to say, but I wasn't bothered. I was concerned for Caz who had to cope with it but as for me – who cares. I was half-way round the world and likely to be for a few more weeks and I couldn't care less. The best thing was though that, after that first night's disaster, Caz had no further trouble with my houses or students.

I have to say that it was this holiday which was the groundbreaker for me. After it I became more laid back, positive, carefree, life was for living, take everything as it comes. I can cope, I can do it. Leave it to me. Nothing phased me.

In the past I was always quite a positive person, but now, I wouldn't let anything get me down. It would be all right. Even when I didn't know what 'it' was, it would still be all right.

In Bombay I found something to rival the Big One at Blackpool Pleasure Beach. Rather than being over in a couple of minutes this usually lasted about forty-five minutes and involved two rickstas. The men get in one and the women in another and you race each other around the outskirts of Bombay. Twelve lanes of traffic and you're up against buses, HGVs, cars, motorbikes etc and they squeeze you in with only millimetres to spare. Because they are open, they're naturally air-conditioned. To race you need the co-operation of the drivers but I never found that to be a problem. They loved it.

They overtake most cars and weave at incredible speed. Forty-five minutes of the biggest highs I've known. Mind boggling.

As we'd drawn nearer to Bombay on the train we began to pass the terrible shanty towns we've all seen on the news programmes. We weren't going too slow so I only got an impression of them.

Since then I've travelled past them so often, sometimes we were even stopped opposite them, I've begun to realize something. The people who occupy them seem to have a rhythm and balance to their life which is possibly missing on some estates in the UK. The top luxury house is made of whole sheets, often blue, of visqueen type heavy polythene. The next down is made up of large torn pieces of various grades of polythene and finally the worst houses are made up of polythene bags fastened together. There are many other levels in between these, but that gives you the idea.

Despite all this the people looked clean and happy. The immaculate wash was laid out on top of mounds of earth, children played around, mothers stood at the doors of their homes chatting to others. There appeared to be a big pot in the centre of a group of houses which was bubbling away. But no matter where you went, even there in the shanties, all the saris and tops matched.

On one occasion, the black-looking stream which runs at the back of the shanties between them and the railway line was host to two different ablutions. At one place a mother was washing her little boy and he was howling as water was poured over his head. Further upstream another older boy, was peeing into the stream. Looking at the state of it, I've a feeling that the urine could have been providing an antiseptic treatment.

As you are probably aware ablutions in India and many other world regions are conducted differently from the UK. The left hand is used instead of toilet paper and there always is running water and a bucket provided in each lavatory. With this in mind, especially with children, I always kept my eye on them once they exited the loo, call it caution, but I wonder how well they had been trained. Had they passed the test? What test? Self preservation tip 85.

To come back to the shanty towns. One thing I will say is that people in India seem to accept their lot. Having done this, they strive to improve it. The people in the shanties were laughing, appeared happy, not how they're always portrayed on documentaries. They looked to have a positive outlook, which is something I would think is not what the programme makers want to get across. I know their lives are hard but they appeared to be coping.

Beggars queue at the temples as the Hindu religion requires worshippers to support the poor. The Hindus

I know take this seriously. Their religion plays an important part in everyday life. Sanjay, only 30, fasts two days per week, Tuesday and Saturday. He only eats in the evenings on those days. Every day before he goes out he makes an offering and says prayers at the little shrine in the apartment.

I had been told that most street beggars only want the money for a drink and not to give them anything. I gave them the benefit of the doubt and hoped I wasn't making the situation worse.

Cyber cafés proliferate along every Indian street I passed. As with all the emerging third world countries, the young in particular, have switched on to the latest technology. They embrace it enthusiastically.

Enterprise I think is a word that was made just to describe Indians. If they can make money from it, however little, they will do it. Offer a service, sell it to you, whatever. They put the same amount of enthusiasm into every sale or deal. It seems like it's a question of honour – and it's in the genes.

One of my photos shows the outside of the block of flats where I stayed. The colourful washing hanging off the balconies gives it an appearance of a Costa hotel where everyone's drying their towels. The only thing missing was the swimming pool.

Dipti's father worked for the government and now he's retired they are very well off by Indian standards. Their apartment is very well appointed and has everything a family needs.

When being given an address in India, it is common for the official address to be detailed as, four doors down from McDonalds, or just left by the co-operative building. Take a right at Mahatma Gandhi Road by the pharmacy. The name Mahatma Gandhi Road seems obvious doesn't it? It's often the longest or one of the most prestigious roads. The name is usually abbreviated to M. G. road.

One of the strangest things I've found in India was that the children, boys, girls, teenagers, would sit in a room with the visitors (whether neighbours or from foreign parts) and quietly listen. They don't fidget, try to interrupt or make a nuisance of themselves in any way. They just sit there and it can be for hours.

I'd worry about this normally if I didn't know that wherever I've been in India the children are considered the most important thing. Everything is for the children so long as they do their homework, they are a VIP.

I think the word I want for Indian youngsters is amenable. I know from Dipti's children that they will occupy themselves quite quietly for some time but also that she showers attention on them some of the time. I'm not saying my children didn't occupy themselves most of the time, but if I think of children in the 21st century in the UK I wonder how an attention deficit disorder child would manage on the sub-continent.

CHAPTER TEN

Fate and a leather elephant

And so to my two-night stay at a chain hotel, Juhu Beach, Bombay. I negotiated as well as I could because I didn't know where I was due to the trip round Bombay which left me totally mystified, I hadn't realized I'd reached the beach where so many Bollywood films are made – Juhu.

I'd already been and enquired at the adjacent Holiday Inn and because of price had chosen the other. Naturally had I realized this was the Holiday Inn at Juhu Beach, where reductions were my due, via American Express. I would have ensconced myself in there where I wouldn't have had to endure the other.

They charged me extra on one night as I needed another bed in each room until Hemman and his wife left the next morning. They charged me through the nose for my phone call, as is usual in hotels, and when I finally ascended to the rooftop swimming pool it seemed like there was no justice in the world.

It was quite late by then as I made my way to the shallow end. Perhaps this was not the best way of describing it. Shallower end was what it was and what it did was come up to my nose when I gratefully cooled myself as I climbed down the ladder.

The look of alarm on my face as I thought I was never reaching the bottom would have made a good still to advertize a horror film, so there I was bobbing. If I didn't bob I would drown and there would be no-one to know until whoever locked up at night found big white mama floating face down and she wouldn't be snorkelling.

Having got my costume wet and cooled off I retreated to my luxury room. This being Bombay I found out that luxury rooms are at a premium and although mine was expensive by Indian standards it was average by Bombay standards. I discovered that on my travels, in Delhi, Cochin, Calcutta and beyond, that Bombay had the most expensive, least satisfactory hotels. Fame had gone to its head. Possibly as the centre for Bollywood movies it felt it could charge London prices. Also, even though Delhi is the capital, Bombay is the financial centre of India.

I dined that night in the restaurant. It was hardly buzzing and rather soulless. The maitre d' was very nice and fussed about me. Very helpful. The food was expensive, but having been cheated by the pool, I was resigned to everything going wrong. So long as the air-conditioning kept going I'd be ok. That would seriously undermine my comfort–zone-at-any-price mentality.

The next morning Hemman and his wife left to conduct business and the rest of us made plans to visit Elephanta Isle. It meant travelling to the Gateway of India (the other side of Bombay) to get a boat out to the island.

I tried, boy how I tried, to make sure we got a fully air-conditioned taxi. It turned into a journey of 1½ hours. I said I'd pay for the taxi. Anything to get air-conditioning. In this case, Sanjay had decided non air-conditioning would do and because he was in charge of the expedition, I didn't realize it was non air-conditioning until we set off. I think it was because he was trying to save me money – but it just could be that as a man he knew better and I was beginning to look like a bloody-minded guest – not an easy guest as was my desire.

When we stopped at traffic lights, beggars descended on us. Some were mutilated, one was covered in lumps and whereas the others had shirts on, he didn't. I suppose this was a selling point in the begging industry and you have to make use of what you've been given. I'm not being cynical or heartless, just practical.

On the way back I was determined to get my way re: air-conditioning and no matter how many cabs we had to let go, I wouldn't give in. I'd seen a sign advertizing air-conditioned cabs and told them to ring it. Shortly after that, it was quite surprising really, we easily found an air-conditioned cab. So I got my wish and found that although I was lovely and cool down to the waist, I was cooking nicely below that. I have since found out that drivers don't like to put on the air-conditioning because it takes more fuel. But surely you pay more for an air-conditioned cab anyway?

It was about midday as we reached the Gateway to India. Although similar to the Arc de Triomphe, it has elements derived from Islamic styles of the 16th century Gujarat. I thought the purchase of a fan of peacock feathers to be judicious at this point. After we'd done the photo calls in front of the Taj Mahal Hotel – a most beautiful and famous building, reminiscent of a palace in the Raj era and the Gateway to India, specially built to commemorate the visit of George the Fifth, we embarked on the boat.

The sea was reasonably calm and I was quite grateful for the breeze. In fact I was pathetically grateful for anything which cooled me. When I'd shown my miniature

Evian water spray (I'd taken 8 with me) to the others, they'd smiled at me, even laughed. Sanjay had dismissed with a superior shake of his head – but I'll tell you something, by the time we were on our return train trip to Valsad, Sanjay was using it as liberally as anyone and this was in second class air-conditioning.

On reaching Elephanta Isle we pulled into the jetty, along with the dozens of other pleasure cruisers, and you could feel the heat beginning to penetrate your skin and the perspiration was answering it quite freely.

We pulled alongside four other boats and because ours was the furthest from the jetty we had to clamber across the old tyres they use to stop the boats banging together or against the harbour. As I crossed the boats they kept separating. This was very alarming for someone who likes to be able to feel the bottom of the swimming pool.

Elephanta Isle is a Hindu religious island with many relics of ancient carved figures in various states of preservation and decay. Mainly in sandstone. There is a statue of a three-faced God called Brahma, who I believe with only one face is normally called Shiva. Monkeys proliferate and although begging are not aggressive even when you get near their young.

I should have realized that there would be a walk. Along a causeway for about 100 yards and then up – yes, up. Very far up. Hills and a great many steps and on each side in the midday sun, a great many stalls. Jewellery, religious objects, cameras, films, hats etc and naturally by every stall, a keen Indian salesman. I should never have stopped to look for a piece of costume jewellery with some of my favourite ruby-coloured stones in. He not only pursued me up the steps but he was waiting for me on the way back down, but by this time he'd assembled every item he could find from his entire stock (and for all I know, all they had on the mainland), which had ruby coloured stones. I only got rid of him when I finally entered a juice bar way beyond the steps. I have to say now, none of the items offered was what I was looking for, otherwise I might have entered negotiations, but to say I felt pressured was putting it mildly.

Although I was with the others, I tended to be ahead of them because Dipti felt obliged to stop at every stall on one side on the way up and the other side on the way down. I wanted to get up as quickly as I could and find shade and down again for the same reason.

On the way back when the others joined me at the bottom of the hill, both Dipti and Barry started serious haggling on a large pair of leather Indian elephants. They were about 18in long, 15in wide and 18in high. They debated whether they could fit them in their luggage. As Dipti is such a serious shopper, needless to say we left the island weighed down by one peacock fan and two leather elephants. I felt quite smug, it's usually me who buys up the place, but I had heavyweight competition from Dipti and realized I wasn't even on her plane.

After waiting in the heat we finally boarded a boat of questionable stability and headed for the mainland. The boat was full of tourists of all nationalities, although predominantly they were Indian. As we approached the harbour I could see many ships, fine looking ships of the Indian Navy at anchor just beyond the jetty. They looked like they were prepared for anything.

We docked at the quayside by the Gateway to India, it was fairly rough and the boat kept moving away from the quay. Sometimes as much as 5 ft appeared between us and it. I was expected to jump. As you may appreciate I may be daft, sorry eccentric, but I'm not stupid. I had visions of the English woman from Valsad disappearing down the side of the boat never to be seen again. My self preservation tip no. 101 came to the fore. I just said, "I'm not jumping that." This 6ft 4in Canadian guy we had been talking to said, "Hold my hand, I'll hold your arm." Barry on the either side, all 5ft 3in of him said "and we'll be fine." So we launched. Well the upshot was everyone else landed and because of my height, my feet landed later than the Canadian and when they touched, I skidded inelegantly and very quickly along the landing stage till someone righted me. But at least I wasn't providing food for the predators of the Indian Ocean who would have thought Diwali had come early with a piece of meat with this much flesh on it.

As I staggered off after the others who looked slightly relieved their guest had managed to return from Elephanta Isle in one piece, Sanjay must have decided a treat was in store. He suggested we get a horse and trap to take us to this restaurant he knew of in the one-way system. It was only a short ride.

There was only one carriage available. It looked slightly listing. Looking back the trip was only about 500 yards maximum which was probably just as well. As the carriage had a bit of a list to start with, it seemed worse as more of us got in. I think if we had-n't had to make a right turn it would have been all right.

We tottered down one side of the Taj Mahal Hotel

block and eventually came to a crossroads, 24 lanes of converging traffic all revving, facing each other, and we needed the one on the right. As we pulled up to await our turn, the driver turned the animal to the right. You notice I said the animal because the carriage part with us on board had a plan of its own. We collapsed to the left, me first followed by Barry, one carved leather elephant, Dipti, Sanjay and another carved leather elephant and oh yes, one peacock fan – it must have been that which did it.

I was balancing upside down with my hands on the roof of a car below me, the others plus elephants pressing upon me. I never thought my fate might be decided by a carved leather elephant. I was just wondering whether clambering onto the roof of the car was my best chance of survival as it would move at the same time as us.

Panic, strangely enough, did not set in, even though I was aware of the 24 lanes waiting for me to be upended in their midst.

But as this is India, nothing is what it seems and as we straightened round the corner so did the carriage and we were all reassembled in our seats as we lurched drunkenly off up the road to our destination, mightily relieved it was on the left.

As we dismounted, with crooked difficulty it has to be said, we were giggling hysterically. It was a relief mechanism and as we stood there the carriage drove off into the night with its list to the left infinitely worse.

The meal at the exclusive restaurant was exquisite and afterwards outside there was a man selling marzipan. It was encased in silver leaf. I tried some. My fillings rebelled, it was like scratching the blackboard.

Despite that, we left refreshed for our hotel. Well, refreshed until we got in the air-conditioned cab, which thank goodness only cooked our nether regions.

CHAPTER ELEVEN

A microcosm of Indian life

We checked out of the hotel the next morning. It cost
£450.00 for two rooms for two nights, two dinners
and ten breakfasts and one phone call. That was one
tenth of the cost of my entire holiday which included
clothes and presents. I have felt entitled to use as
much of their notepaper as possible. I even felt it
should be edged in gold leaf and encrusted with a few
diamonds for good measure.

We were due to take the train in the afternoon so it
was decided we should go shopping. By now, I was
insisting on rickstas. One for the girls, one for the
boys. Natural air-conditioning. Rickstas are not
allowed to go into the centre of Bombay. Only taxis.
They must think it makes the centre seem classier. It
may, but it's not as exciting.

So there I was, shopping at the street markets in the
Bombay outskirts, my feet swollen, sore, hot and dusty
in the midday sun. I'm sure there's a song warning
me not to do it, but I was being organized and I didn't
want to be a party pooper. I only found out when we
got back, the whole trip to Bombay had been arranged
for my benefit!

Despite what you might think, even out of the large
cities, life in any town seems to be at a frighteningly
fast pace. So after our shopping spree we approached
the station at Bandra on the outskirts where Sanjay
once again negotiated for us. This time to have our
own second-class air-conditioned compartment, baksheesh was required. The station itself was busy, hot

and as usual dusty. I wondered if I'd ever be allowed to do this for myself. Did I want to? It was made to seem complicated.

I've now realized air-conditioning is never really needed as all trains usually have their windows wide open. For most of the four hours I travelled with my head out of the window greedily taking in everything unfolding before my eyes.

A river we crossed about an hour out of Bombay was typical of the way these things are used by everyone. Women were washing clothes on some of the stones on the edge and even some part way across. Despite the monsoons just finishing this part of the river was very low with grassy little islands, boulders sticking up from shallow waters and where it seemed to be deeper, it was still shallow enough for a driver to be washing his ricksta. Cows a bit further up were drinking, children swimming, shrieking, playing games. It seemed all human life was there. A microcosm of Indian domestic life. If there'd been a kiosk on one bank, a bureau de change on the other, it would have summed up India without my having to explain it. One picture could tell the whole story.

As we boarded the train another left the station and it was what I would call an Indian train. People two deep were hanging out of all the doors, and as it picked up speed there was no sign their journey would not be conducted in the doorway.

The Indians are not the tidiest of people, streetwise anyway. Their homes are fine, but outside it's as though there is a law demanding that they drop a certain amount of litter each year to maintain the status quo. Without it, the animals might starve.

So at the station the space in between the lines was

festooned with litter. Now whereas in Britain, pigeons and sparrows make up our station scavengers, in India it's usually the pig. He snuffles up and down and being a sensible Indian pig, he knows where's safe and when the trains are due. Birds do their bit as well, some dogs, but pigs seem to have the railway franchise sewn up.

On the journey we stopped at a few main stations. This was an opportunity for sellers of all manner of goodies to come to the windows, even enter the train, to tempt you. Dipti, forever the shopper, bought some fruit. The woman selling it peeled it for her, deposited it on a card and gave it to her. Now this is what you're told not to do as any manner of dreaded lurgies can be passed on this way. Dipti offered me a piece. By now I was getting blasé and risked one piece. Later on Dipti told me that we'd go and visit the peacock apartment soon.

Once we set off again a man selling nuts appeared. You ordered what you wanted. Once again these were manhandled, but not before he'd got out an old-fashioned brass weighing scale and all the weights and meticulously weighed your purchase.

Sanjay then went to bed. He mounted to the top 'bunk', a luggage rack in our compartment and went to sleep. I'm always amazed at the way some Indians can just switch off. And he hadn't even practised yoga before this – well at least he didn't do anything obvious.

Shortly before our destination, Sanjay reappeared. He said yes to a shoe wallah. The man polished them a bit and then in the gangway, sitting cross-legged, got out all his little tools and began to sew the side and upper together. He was a bit bigger than Rumpelstiltskin, but the image came to mind. He finished off with a polish again which you could see your face in. Sanjay paid him 14p (10 rupees).

10 rupees was what I have been using to give beggars. I now realized that meeting 5 people a day like me would given them the average wage for someone working hard in a factory for 8 hours or more. I just felt so stingy only giving one rupee. It's only much later that I realized this was fairer to the hard-working Indian. To disabled or mutilated or obviously sick I would always give 10 rupees. Dipti says the hairdresser in Valsad only charges 10 rupees for a haircut. They hope to average 10 a day, double the average wage.

I've noticed that TV's are around £100.00. No wonder they're such a prized item. Barry said that when Indians buy electrical or luxury goods they leave the price on so friends and neighbours can see how much they've paid for them. I suppose if the average wage is under £1.00 per day, it must be the second job which pays for them. I kid you not, many Indians, even in this heat, have second jobs.

IT managers only earn (in 2000) about £100 per month after taxes. No wonder so many want to emigrate. UK, Canada and the US are favourite. Most likely because of the common language.

So back to our arrival back in Valsad from our Bombay excursion. Dad had got a ricksta waiting for us. Because of the law, anyone with more than 3 people in has to use the back roads to and from the centre, in case the police see you. So I've been illegal in India – quite a few times in fact. Makes me feel a backpacking moment coming on.

Our meal was ready as we arrived back and I gratefully ate up as quickly as I could. It was 9.00pm and I felt, due to the mad dogs and Englishwoman at midday in Bombay, plus the 4 hour train journey, I could be forgiven for making an early exit.

Dipti came up to me excitedly saying that we were going to a dance (in my honour) if I wasn't too tired. Tired? Me? Swollen ankles, me? Get dressed up in pink silk sari on loan from Mama and appear downstairs in the garage as soon as possible? Of course. I'm the ideal guest.

There was great excitement as I was arrayed in my finery. The pink of my sari couldn't compete though with the pink of my complexion – I have photos to prove it. I'd tried on different saris, but I think even they'd realized I could be a rather large grease spot on the floor if it continued. They kept assuring me I was the guest of honour, but I think it was a ploy to make sure I went.

Dipti put on her extremely fine sari in cream and navy blue satin with lace inserts. Barry dressed up. I know I was guest of honour but this was looking serious. Were they expecting a VIP? Well no, the dance had a religious theme. Dipti and Barry were presenting the offerings and it was duly camcorded by Sanjay, who had appeared in a cream silk salwar kameez man-type outfit. I have asked Dipti for the name but she just says it's something like that. Evidently he knew why he needed a kip on the Bombay-Valsad Express. Unfortunately I didn't.

It was explained to me that the dance was to be in the underground car park. On entering via the lift I found a small temple or shrine had been erected just by the lift. There were pictures and statues of Sai Baba and flower garlands and fruit had been arranged around them. A carpet was spread and two men sat on it playing instruments. Holy songs were sung and Barry and Dipti approached with their offerings. The whole ceremony took about 20 minutes. Neighbours and friends from all over came and as I say, Sanjay recorded the event.

Afterwards the shrine was tidied away and the music continued for the dance. There must have been about 75 people there including children. Dipti's mother had made food and there were soft drinks. I had the ubiquitous water bottle to hand. Sunstroke was never far away.

Sunstroke in a ground level car park. Well, all right, heatstroke. Same difference.

Being guest of honour didn't just mean being introduced to everyone who hadn't already met me. Roughly translated it meant everyone looked at me when I was trying to follow the dance. I got looks of incredulity, curiosity, sympathy and encouragement.

Everyone who was anyone in the area was there. Doctors, lawyers, office workers, all the women (housewives automatically) and dozens of children. All these children including the very young ones of about two to three years could do the dance in a more co-ordinated fashion than white mama.

One very distinguished looking man, oozing authority, took me in hand and tried to get me to follow the rhythm of what I now realize is one of the simpler dances. I think he felt obliged to do this as I was likely to trip him up, assault him or dislocate his back as he fell over me if left to my own devices.

The dances normally take the form of a big circle so eventually there is a hypnotic rhythmic beat to it. This naturally was without the guest of honour fouling it up. I purposefully missed the stick dance, I felt I'd inflicted as much pain/damage as goodwill would allow on the good citizens of Valsad. It's true to say I danced my heart out, but the Corps de Ballet needn't worry.

I was introduced to Ranee's mother and sister. They

had come across town. This is one of the few things Ranee can attend so soon after the birth.

I was in a permanent state of perspiration, sitting out every other dance, due to concentration, determination and the fact that it was 85° at midnight plus heaven knows what humidity. I'd even had to wear mosquito repellent.

I finally piked off about 12.30am feeling I'd done my bit to cement or destroy Anglo-Indian relations for the next generation. And the worst of it was, Barry had it all on camcorder. The only redeeming feature was I was not likely to be highlighted on TV the next day.

Next morning Barry's video was the thing to watch. I noticed I still looked hot, but not as bad as that first day – I'd felt about 110. I also noticed that when they started a leaping about dance I sat that one out – me and my water. Self-preservation tip No. 732.

The video Barry took of our arrival followed and now I can see why everyone kept offering me a chair. I look extremely warm, in fact a little bit longer and I could probably be served rare with a Yorkshire Pudding.

As I said, at the dance I didn't look as bad, so perhaps I was adjusting. Dipti's aunts and uncles who were at the house when I arrived have asked me to visit them. One couple live in Surat, miles away and the other couple live not too far from there.

As neither couple speak any English and my Gujarati is still confined to the necessities of life – thank you, please, I'm full up, I'm fine, how are you? – it was felt Dipti and Barry would have to accompany me. I wasn't sure if I'd have time left at the end and I don't know if this fit in with Dipti's plans. We'd have to see.

By then I'd decided to extend my four weeks to six weeks. I'd started making my escape plans. I wouldn't have to tunnel out but it was going to be very difficult as all sorts of obstacles were being put in my way.

CHAPTER TWELVE

Room for the Edinburgh Tattoo

When you take to the roads in India, by foot or in any vehicle, as I said before you take your life in your hands. It's as though everyone presumes they have a charmed life. You feel like you've entered another world. Well of course you have. The whole of India is another world – a seriously fascinating world.

Dipti, Barry, Sanjay and I were going to Goa for four days. We'd been to the air-conditioned travel agents with Dipti's father (remember they're not allowed out on their own) and negotiations had begun. This took about an hour and I believe money was saved but I've begun to think it's like a double glazing salesman, where it's added on before it's taken off. Just for honour's sake.

At the agents I then mooted that I would like to travel to Rajasthan via four star hotels. This did not go down well. The agent told me he couldn't arrange for me to go to the hotels I had on my list but he could arrange some good hotels which Indians used. At this point in my travels, I was still clinging to my standards and my demands with my customary determination. Dipti's father wasn't too sure either about my going. It was dangerous. Barry said it was dangerous – Dipti thought it was dangerous. Cheeky Indians. Yes, but how cheeky? You mean it's not like England – where if I walk out in a major city after dark I will be mugged or raped? This got better by the minute. Surely, cheeky didn't mean they'd murder you?

We finally left the agents and returned home. A

cooling juice from Happiness was called for. I tackled Barry again about returning to the agents to arrange for me to travel after Goa and return just before they left for the UK. I don't think this went down very well and more obstacles were put in my way. It was about now that I felt if I'd been field-trained by the Paras I'd have been better equipped to deal with this. But sheer bloody-mindedness kicked in.

It's not as if I was staying in fleapits. I was not going overnight on a train. I reckoned the only place of real risk was railway stations and airport arrivals. In most cases, I would arrange to be picked up by the hotel. It's just commonsense really. Like counting the number of pieces of luggage you've got all the time. Most people though are friendly and helpful. You could come up against rogues etc. travelling at railway stations in England, especially Victoria and Euston.

Anyway, the upshot was, at this stage I didn't care if I was "done" by a porter, taxi or ricksta. I'd negotiate but only so far; we were talking 4p or 5p sometimes. It wasn't worth the hassle. Big travel and hotels was where the money went. So long as I wasn't robbed or "set upon" as they say, it was ok. Anyway Amex had me insured. It'd just be inconvenient.

So Barry and I went back to the agents. The only thing we finalized were the details for Goa and because I was a foreigner I had to pay an extra supplement—somewhere around £20.00, which didn't worry me. Including the flight from Bombay, it was around £120.00 including full board. I had nothing to do with these negotiations and was just going with the flow. It sounded ok. I wondered what we'd get for that as the flight was £80.00. We would go in four days time.

Dipti's reason for coming home now was to return

to a temple up in the hills and conduct a ceremony for the safe arrival of her child five years before. She takes her religion very seriously, as do all her family and the trip was planned for the next day, so I was being shipped out to an hotel with swimming pool, by the sea, fully inclusive for £10.00 per day at Daman, the liquor store town, to stay for one night, but I'd opted for two. I couldn't wait.

I was soon delivered to my hotel. The first room I got had air-conditioning that smelt like a snake had died, then the rat that came to scavenge it died and the cat that came for the rat followed the same fate. This second room was only slightly better, but I was only there 2 days and I couldn't be bothered checking out the whole complex.

The manager was a very nice man and asked would I join him one lunchtime. He would love to go to England. There he would work 14 hour days. In India, because of the heat, that was more or less impossible. He had been an hotel manager for quite a while, starting after university. His English was very good.

Daman it appeared was a training centre for many Brits and Europeans and was about one hour from Valsad by car. I didn't see any other Europeans in Valsad, but no-one stared and appeared to notice me.

The manager in Daman couldn't have been more helpful and friendly. He seemed to like to have someone to speak to about world affairs and economies and boring though it might sound, these were things close to my heart.

So, many businessmen were using the hotel and one awkward incident involved an Indian one. I was swimming in the pool. An Indian family had been in at the same time. The woman was wearing an ordinary swimming costume as was I, but eventually there I was on my own in the pool.

The Indian man brought a chair and placed it by the steps where I had to leave the pool. There was enough room for me to do a Venus rising from the waves, but only just. I kept on swimming but realized I was going to have to leave before he moved. He was there for the duration.

As I left the pool, I had to squeeze past his chair and he was staring at me quite rudely. Now I'm not prudish, but I felt distinctly uncomfortable under his gaze.

Racing through my mind were all types of thoughts. Should I push him in and watch him sink? Should I call him a pervert and see if I deciphered a blush? Should I just ask why he was sitting just there? As it was, English reserve won, well nearly. I stared at him icily, sneered slightly and looked at his crotch. It seemed safer than pushing him in. Who knows what law I might have broken doing that? And I haven't forgotten the air-conditioned men's department at that store or the poor women and children waiting on the narrow, stifling stairs. At this point I wasn't sure what status white women had in this society. Were we higher or lower than the men. Were we higher or lower than the women? How far up the caste system was I?

The hotel had an aura of vastness, not least because the floors on exiting the lift were gargantuan. Large pillars were spaced throughout, half a dozen sofas were scattered about and there was still room for the Edinburgh Tattoo. From the brochure the four star restaurant offered Chinese, Punjabi, Seafood and Moghal amongst others. Somewhere in the grounds was a "Disco-theque" called Hell which I'm pleased to say I never found or more importantly, it never found me.

This was my first chance for independence up against the cheeky Indians. My eager anticipation was similar to childbirth. Was it as bad as everyone made out? Just how bad could it be?

So with this curiosity in mind I negotiated with a ricksta wallah to take me to the Post Office and sight-seeing. In Valsad, Dipti's Dad had gone to get one for me. Nice, but no independence.

It was, as is usual for me, about lunchtime when I hit the Post Office queue to have my letter weighed. There is no gum on the back of Indian envelopes and I've now found out that they staple them. Yes, all the way through the letter as well.

Arriving at the Post Office I found myself outside as the queue was quite long. The sun was overheating me beautifully. Not only was I the only European, I was the only woman. It appears that the Post Office is man's work. It is outside the home.

After about one minute there was a muttering and the men queuing told me to go to the front of the queue. At first I wasn't sure. I stepped forward hesitantly. They kept beckoning me forward until I was at the counter. A clerk weighed the letter, charged me and I was out. I said thank you to everyone as I left.

I haven't worked out if allowing me to the front was because I was (a) a foreigner, (b) a woman, (c) they were collecting their dole or (d) they'd seen my dance on TV and knew I needed all the help I could get.

I set off on my sightseeing tour of Daman. At this stage I hadn't known that it felt, in that part of India colonized by the Portuguese, like Goa and Kerala. We went down to the river where a wooden sign at the bridge stated that Leprosy can be cured. The port and accompanying houses looked quite prosperous and attractive, if quaint, but I noticed as a fishing boat churned up the silt that there was rust-red sediment, quite a violent colour, dyeing the water. When this happened the water turned a dark tan colour. It didn't look too healthy.

We stopped at an ancient fort and lighthouse used by the Portuguese. I stayed as long as the midday sun allowed but on return the ricksta was nice and breezy as we tootled along.

The driver pointed out the part of town belonging to the Muslim population. It was a leafy lane just as you entered town. Children were playing, wives were going about their chores, there was no sign of the men.

He then offered to take me to an old church. As we turned down the lane leading to this, a snake slithered across the road, too quick for me and my camera. I've no idea what type it was, greenish in colour – now there's a surprise – about 6 feet long. It was going from the ditch on one side of the road to the other. If I got any nearer to one on my trip, I'm relieved to say I never found out.

The church was very old and quaint. It looked European and I presumed it was Catholic, but now realize it could have belonged to the Coptic Christians. St Thomas the Apostle, he of the doubtful thoughts, was said to have arrived on the Indian mainland and started a Christian Church there. Whatever, the church was very peaceful and I lit my candle.

After this I asked to go to the beach and would the driver collect me in one hour. Had I had enough training to cope with being left exposed to cheeky

Indians and danger for one hour? It would seem so.

I was near a café, in case my water ran out and there were lots of different people offering seaside things, Indian style. There was a family with coconuts just waiting to machete them for you. Another with two young girls, aged about 12, selling jewellery. Another kiosk selling coke and other drinks and finally on the beach, young boys only about 12 offering camel rides in the surf. The trouble was as the camels disturbed the sand, bright orange swirls appeared in the surf. Was this the most polluted sea in the world or did it just look like it?

Anyway, that was the main reason I didn't venture for even a paddle. This was the Arabian Sea and I wanted to say I'd been in it, but at what price? Not this. I was duly collected after an hour and allowing this was my first adventure into the unknown, I was quite relieved to get back. Who knew what real dangers lurked out there. I'd been warned, oh how I'd been warned.

Dipti, her father, his friend – with a car – Barry, Benita and Priscilla collected me the next day. We then went to another hotel for a meal by the beach, with the waves crashing and finally made our way home. The next day was to be Goa. I asked would we be able to visit the peacock apartment?

On arrival back at their apartment I found Mum had erected a shrine, with banana leaves as decoration, garlands of marigolds, the Hindus favourite holy flower, and food offerings. A hammock was overhead and the furniture had been rearranged. So this was the reason we'd eaten out.

A holy man was visiting and the women and children were coming to hear him. It would take about two hours. I retreated to the cool of my bedroom to read and eventually to have a siesta. Dipti came and told me when it was over. The holy man had been instructing everyone.

We had a quiet evening and got packed for Goa. I found it strange we weren't taking the girls but they were happy to stay with their grandparents, also Sanjay's wife Ranee wasn't allowed to travel yet, but I noticed that women weren't always included in social arrangements. It's a man's world in India but here was one bolshi Northern Brit about to exert her influence for the benefit of womankind everywhere. Independent India here I came. And I still hadn't visited the woman and her peacock. I wondered how big her apartment was?

CHAPTER THIRTEEN

Goa and beyond

The family were making arrangements for me to be back for Diwali October 26th as there'd be celebrations. The house would be decorated with garlands and coloured lights as in the UK. A big difference there was that all the garlands were of marigolds festooning the walls and even pictures. I think it was their version of holly.

I wondered how I could get back for Diwali as it was already the 14th. It only gave me 12 days and I'd got big plans. Dipti kept talking about Sanjay and herself accompanying me to Rajasthan. This would be fine by me but I did intend to stay four star whilst I was there. A decision would be made whilst we were in Goa. I've told them I'm going via American Express agents so let them dare lose me or have some other mishap befall me.

We were dropped at the railway station. I had 3 cases; I'd only left one at the apartment. The others were travelling lighter – ah yes, but did they have the ambitious plans I had now the cell door had been left ajar?

We took the usual trip, four hours to Bombay. I knew better by now and always wore my sunglasses as I leant my head against the window grill. The pollution was so bad, I could hardly see the first time I made the trip. It took my eyes about 6 hours to recover.

At one of the stops a little girl entered the train. She had a broom made of the usual malleable branches.

She looked about 7 or 8 but could just as easily have been 10. She was dressed in a sari and she silently swept out the compartment and put out her hand. Sanjay, our postmaster general, gave her a rupee but didn't really look at her. I wondered what her place was in the caste system but in the usual repressed English way I didn't like to ask.

I noticed she got off at the next stop to wait I presume for the next train. I wondered how safe she was and where her family were.

So we arrived in Bombay for the midday sun. Having two men with me meant I was not in charge of most of my luggage, which was just as well as the hike up the platform began to resemble a route march. Indian trains are so long.

As we left I saw a train just pulling out. It was packed with men standing, hanging out the door, once again at least two deep. They were laughing and seemed to regard it as normal. It was the sort of scene you often see depicted in films of India. They looked carefree, but do you think they'd look so if they knew the month before many people had been killed travelling just so and on the top of the train when it went through a low tunnel? Thinking about it they probably would, based on the premise, it can't happen to me. Nearly all the trains have horizontal grills on the usually opened windows, which make them look like prisons and as though they are the cattle-trucks from hell. Inside though it's a different story. Most carriages are comfortable, reasonably clean but dusty. First class air conditioned, are always clean, rarely dusty. By now I'd been in every class but third. I've been air-conditioned, non-air-conditioned, both in first and second. To be honest, I don't see much difference except for first class air-conditioned, and then only on the train in Kerala. The rest seem much of a muchness.

We piled into two rickstas and raced against each other to the airport. Once again it didn't take much to get the drivers to be willing participants in this dice with death – but remember I wasn't meant to die yet or the road to hell would have got me.

Check-in completed, we had two hours to kill and as we arrived at the airport I saw a sign for Indian airlines. I told Dipti I was just going to see what they had. By the time she joined me I was just paying for a 21 day excursion ticket called "Discover India" and that is just what I intended to do. I could go anywhere (in one direction) I wanted and I had the ticket dated for the first flight out of Goa in 6 days time. My wings were just beginning to spread and I was thundering down the road ready for take off to soar over Kerala, Rajasthan and anywhere else my fancy took me. I was feeling good – really good and dying to find out just what this danger was that I would be in It had to be somewhere after all the warnings.

Whilst I was waiting to be served, they had the sensible ticket queuing system, I noticed an electronic ticker tape that said, "Tourists paying in US Dollars, discounts". When it was my turn I enquired. The lady had no idea what it meant, so asked her manager. This lady thought it could be the 15 day excursion for $500.00. I thought about this and asked had they any longer, which was when the 21 day reared its head for $750.00. This was about £500.00 and seemed good value.

It meant I would only return for 2 days before we left but gave me 3 weeks after Goa to cover the areas I wanted. Dipti looked impressed and anxious. When they'd been trying to stop my travelling before I explained I had brought up 5 children, run 2 companies of my own, was currently running my third and had somehow survived and no matter what they thought, I would survive in India. They looked doubtful.

We returned to the main airport and had just got to the security check – we were actually going through to the departure lounge – when Sahara Airways and a jobsworth decided I couldn't fly. I had not paid the surcharge demanded of foreigners. So I was hauled back, the others followed.

Dipti, Barry and Sanjay explained it had been paid to the travel agent in Valsad. Jobsworth explained it did not show on the ticket. Since I hadn't seen these tickets I couldn't argue. Dipti said she would contact the agent. The agent promised to ring her back. He didn't, she tried his colleague in Bombay. Lunchtime – no answer. An hour later and our flight time was almost ready. Then I saw a different side to polite little Dipti from England. Here was a bolshi, foul-mouthed Dipti from Valsad. I have to hasten to add that when she lived in Valsad originally I don't think she knew these words. But now I think f****** b*****d crossed her lips when speaking to the travel agent.

In the meantime I had politely gone and asked the official if progress were being made. He said very curtly, "I'm waiting". Very dismissive. So, after an hour of Indian intransigence, I'd had enough, the flight to Goa would be leaving without me in 20 minutes.

Leaving the others sitting miserably, I went over once again and asked him what was happening, the same rudeness, so I flipped. Now all my family will know what that means and sometimes ducking is required.

I said to him in something between a hiss and a British Raj voice "That's it. I've had enough, there must be some way round this and I'm ready for knocking heads together and going to see the airport manager."

Jobsworth became really nice and when Dipti and Sanjay, looking ever more miserable, went to phone again, he gave me back my boarding card and wished me a pleasant journey. I asked if he'd heard anything, he hadn't but he said he trusted me. It's surprising what a blunt Northerner can do with a few well chosen words.

I smiled at him, his reward for coming to his senses, and as the others joined me I told them not to worry about me. I'd manage – believe you me, I would.

Suddenly I realized, these scare stories were all in the mind, just like childbirth. You need to try something first before you believe everything everyone tells you.

I found Indians themselves were cautious, bureaucracy scared them, problems were insurmountable. They'd sit and wheeler-deal, show you how it should be done and they had saved £3.00 and it had taken an hour. Even in air-conditioning I couldn't be bothered, though I know £3.00 means more to some of the local people than to me. My verdict though was that the agent was a dingbat (the most polite word I could use). I felt it in Valsad and the airport debacle confirmed it.

Now I'm not the first and I won't be the last, but I thought Goa was an island off the coast of India. This could stem from the fact that (a) I'd never visited Goa before and (b) I'd had not the faintest interest in India, despite doing Clive of India for 'O' Level. The number of people I've spoken to since who thought the same thing is amazing. It's probably because it's described as being on Goa, not in Goa.

Our hotel was on Vagator Beach. Well actually our bungalow was at the beach, the reception, swimming pool, restaurant and library were up 71 long winding steps about half a mile away.

Dipti and I shared one bungalow, Sanjay and Barry another. If I only wanted to go on the beach this would be perfect. Unfortunately I needed to eat and swim.

There was one English couple there but the rest were Indians. One family had travelled from Calcutta by train, quite a long journey. They had come for 4 weeks. Makes sense if you've come so far. The daughter was 13 and she gave me her e-mail address. How come 13 year olds in third world countries have e-mail and I had to admit I didn't have one then?

I've noticed that if you ask for something to be done, the answer is usually "immediately". But if it's done before you check out, it's unusual. When we discovered that 415 and 416 keys opened each other, I stood over them, whilst they changed them.

Once again it's £10.00 per day inclusive and although it's ok for the money, it's not luxurious. This is what the agent thought was suitable. This was why he couldn't find me the hotels to book I was looking for. Either that or he was under instructions to create an obstacle course. Fortunately, all obstacles can be walked round.

The heat was very oppressive, even at the sea. I was struggling, but not as much as Dipti whose face was swelling on the lips with all the sun. She had been in the pool a lot. Barry swam but mainly sat by it sunbathing. He wanted to tan. No comment.

Vagator Beach and its next door neighbour Anjuna were still quiet, even though the hippies started there on Goa in the 60's. This was just the beginning of the season and the sea was not yet blue. The monsoons were still affecting it. At least another week or two before it changed. There was so much sand in the water, it looked like the colour of the Blackpool sea.

I've had my own lizard as well. It wasn't Dipti's, it was mine. It had also lost the end of its tail. Actually that could have been me when I opened the bathroom door, it liked lurking in door frames.

I'd got used to the electricity going off. Every room had candles and matches and at first you wondered why. One night at dinner it went off four times. You just hoped you'd been served your hot food before it went off, otherwise it was candles at the ready as you all sat talking, drinking water and wondering just how long the romantic atmosphere continued whilst your stomach rolled. It would appear the electricity failed for up to 15 minutes a time on a regular basis just to keep the locals on their toes.

Whilst I chatted to the 13 year old from Calcutta she told me she was at school in Darjeeling. She said it was very beautiful and I remembered it was a hill station for the Raj to escape the summer heat of Calcutta. It sounded perfect for me. Escaping the heat. Three beautiful words.

The next day after our arrival, the other three went to the market. Dipti needed her shopping fix and Indian men are used to going to carry things. I felt quite sick at the thought of shopping in a hot market and travelling in a non-air-conditioned car. I would stay by the pool or the beach.

I was on the beach late afternoon. I like it better as it begins to cool. A young boy and his cool bag approached. I bought a can of coke. I'd no money with me but told him I'd bring it, same time next day. He trusted me. The walk back to the bungalow was at least 100 yards and that would defeat the object of buying the coke.

We chatted for a bit and he was saving for his education. He wanted to go to university. He looked about 15, but once again, I wasn't sure. He wandered off. Business would be slow, there weren't many people around. Then came a group of ladies with sarongs. I explained I'd no money and they went on their way laughing good naturedly.

Then they arrived. Bang on 4.00pm. The cows of Vagator Beach. So famous – although I didn't know then, – that they featured on a postcard. Well I got my pictures. They wandered down and sat chewing their cud. It doesn't matter whether it's the third lane of a ring road or a hippie beach, a cow has to do . . .

Dipti returned from the market with two sarongs for me, one silk, one cotton. It had been hot she assured me, making me even more glad I'd discovered the beach.

The next day, I duly appeared at the beach late afternoon, bought another can of coke and settled my bill. The young lad came into view at exactly the same time. He got home from school, loaded up his cool bag, put in the ice and he was down. I suppose it beats a paper round in the drizzle.

With all that I'd learned in my short time away from Valsad, an idea was forming in my head, two more days in Goa as the plane for Cochin (Kochi) only went every few days and then one week in Kerala and the canals, one week Darjeeling and the Himalayas and one week Rajasthan.

I spent many happy hours in the air-conditioned coolness of our bungalow with maps and tour guide books – well I didn't want to miss anything. The enormous map of India was spread over Dipti's bed. I had trouble finding Darjeeling. There it was, stuck in a tiny bubble which appeared between Bhutan, Tibet, Nepal and Bangladesh. Above it was Sikkim province.

I could see if I went in a big circle I would cover a lot of the edges of India, but not the centre. That would have to wait for another trip. There I was never wanting to come, now, if only in my mind, planning another trip. A friend, Anne, who had travelled widely, a great deal of it with her job, said of all the countries she visited, India was the one which affected her the most. You would never forget it. It stayed with you. Of course she was right. I don't know if it was the sheer diversity, the energy of the people or the many faces which were presented to you in so short a space of time, but it had something.

As I made my plans, other than the feeling that I was embarking on an adventure into the unknown against the better judgement of the locals, adrenaline was giving me the feeling that I could do anything. Anything I put my mind to. Anything I wanted. The world was not only my oyster, it could be my lobster as well.

As I planned, I picked up one guide book after the other. These were kept in a pile by my bed. As I finished with each one I discarded it back into the pile. Now my gecko liked to hide in the books as I found out as I threw the first one down. I startled it and it shot out from under my Fodors Guide Book as my

Lonely Planet landed.

Trouble was, in this case, neither it nor I learned very quickly and I kept picking them up and throwing them down and every single time it shot out.

The morning I was leaving, I checked under my puzzle book, no lizard, picked up the rest and who should shoot under my sheets after being launched from my Foders but my friend. I uncovered it and it stayed quite still whilst I talked to it. (I aimed for a 2 month old baby intellect) and got my camera. The flash didn't scare it, after all this was a being used to losing its tail in extremis, so I put my hand behind it and aimed the camera with the other. It looks quite a miserable specimen on my photos but as this was the first gecko I'd had any meaningful relationship with, this was a seminal moment.

CHAPTER FOURTEEN

The hammer and sickle of Kerala

Dipti, Barry and Sanjay left for the airport. She'd promised we'd visit the peacock lady when I got back. That was probably a carrot to get me back. I ordered a taxi to take me to the Holiday Inn Resort further south in Goa. This was the hotel I'd chosen as having the best deal for two more nights. It was £30 inclusive of food but in comparison with the other it was a palace. A shared room would only be £20.00 per night so really it was just double the price of my last hotel. It was all on the level, the swimming pool was 4 ft deep nearly all over. As someone who wouldn't go out of her depth, this was ideal.

Although I was on my own now, I wasn't really. I mean what could happen to me in a 4 Star hotel? I wasn't even leaving the grounds.

On the way to the hotel we'd passed through some lovely countryside and there was a sign proclaiming the entrance to Infant Jesus Farm. Further along there was the Sacred Heart of Jesus Farm. It makes names like Holly Bank Farm and Miles End Farm seem a trifle mundane not to say lacking in imagination. Does a farm dedicated to Jesus do better than a farm named after a rather prickly shrub?

They had a disco at the hotel, though I never heard it. The nice thing was though, a quartet played in the reception area every night. There was a massage which I thought I'd have the next day, but that day I was having a dress copied. I was paying the boutique £13.00 and I think I could have got it for £10.00, but I couldn't be bothered haggling. I'd also taken them a blouse of mine with a tear in it and told them to do that for me as well. He looked quite surprised, probably not used to cheeky foreigners, how dared we usurp the privilege of the locals? Thought it was only themselves who took advantage.

I noticed there was a candle and matches in the room. Doesn't breed confidence in the electricity system. Their enthusiasm to do something, even something advertized, is often not supported by the actual undertaking. In the case of my dress, it was appalling. Too big seams, too chunky. I took my blouse and refused to pay for the dress. Told them I was leaving the next morning so it had to be ready by then. I never heard from them again. Having seen the proposed garment, I wasn't sorry.

Although the electricity went off three times whilst I was there, it was never off for more than about a minute. As though a generator had kicked in or similar. Anyway, it never inconvenienced me. I ventured to the beach one day and even though there were many trees to shade me, I still found it extremely hot and quickly made my way back to the 4ft bliss of the swimming pool. The sea water was still brown coloured. As the seas calmed, blue would appear.

This was only a staging post. I knew it and I felt it. Tomorrow was when it would start for real. Although I am writing this with hindsight, I had no idea what would happen to me once I was no longer protected by either Indians or gateways.

I intended presenting myself as soon as I'd taxied in from the airport to the American Express agent in Cochin. Surely he'd look after me? Throw enough money at him and it would be ok. That was the theory anyway.

I had already booked into the Malabar Residency Hotel, Cochin, which was opposite a big green with a Catholic Church at one end. As I arrived cricket was being played on the green by youngsters. I'd flown from Goa to Cochin and taken the long journey into the city. Hammer and sickles were everywhere. On walls, on buildings. I'd never thought of India like this. During the ride we had to stop at a level crossing. It was still manually operated. One thing India has is plenty of manpower.

We were the first car in the queue and as we waited with the barriers down, a scooter came alongside. The woman passenger got off and walked through the pedestrian gates. The scooter driver limboed under the barrier with his bike, engine still running. She re-mounted and they were off again. Neither I nor the driver said anything.

After quite a time the train passed and the man came out and opened the gates. He then proceeded to place a dark red banner about 7ft wide, 2ft deep, across the main track. I presume this was meant stop to any oncoming trains. After the mess of our railways who am I to poke fun at another country and their safety efforts?

I checked in at my hotel. As I approached the reception desk I saw a swimming pool, just adjacent to the lobby and at the far end a Hindu Shrine decorated of course with marigolds. There was a brass stand about three feet high in front of it with oil burning in it. I was on the ground floor, my room was beautiful and simple and led out to my own garden with its table and chairs. The hotel used to be the Governor's residency and it showed.

I immediately took the cab back across the river to downtown and was deposited at the door of the offices of the Great India Tour Company, American Express Agent.

The title appealed to my sense of things to come. Adventure, mystery, in fact an Agatha Christie type of name. It conjured up images of Rajahs, elephants, tigers and Royal trains. Luggage, bound with metal strips being stowed by turbaned servants or employees of the Great Companies, organizing, scurrying, lifting, to get you on your way. All this from one title. It was all there.

The owner of the company introduced himself, realized I'd come to pay for not only my holidays but for his own for the next few years. Naturally, he was most pleasant.

Due to the danger, I asked him to arrange for me a week in Kerala, where I would be ferried about via private drivers between locations. Also, could he book something in the Himalayas for me? This proved a bit of a problem as he had to contact another agent for this. Evidently the Great India Tour Company was happiest arranging the south of the country.

I've decided the 21 day Discover India ticket will be used fully.

Eventually I left having got 7 nights arranged at three different hotels. I was to be met at the railway station at Thiranthapuran (used to be Trivandrum) by a taxi and taken to my hotel at Samudra. I was taking a train from Cochin to Thiranthapuran as I could not leave Cochin twice by plane and I was coming back that way to the Himalayas. Anyway it would give me a chance to see some more of the countryside and travel independently on a train.

Since I had decided on my own grand tour, I also had to change my Singapore Airline ticket for a later one. At their office in Cochin they were really helpful and for the first and only time in my life I was not charged anything to alter the dates. Bliss.

On my return to my hotel, I had dinner. Mr. Francis, the manager asked might he join me. We got on really well. He'd been a senior manager for the Taj group of hotels and the German who bought the Residence tempted him and at great risk to his career, he joined him at the Malabar, six months before completion of renovations. It would appear this has worked out as it's now known as a Stealth Wealth Hotel where celebrities go for peace and quiet. Mr Francis didn't tell me this I read it in one of the glossy magazines on my bedroom table. It was a peaceful place to visit, however briefly, and he was a lovely man. The next morning I was given a complimentary jeep to the railway station, which was a nice gesture.

I was disappointed that I couldn't visit more of Cochin, there was a large Jewish quarter, the largest in India. Been there for centuries. Cochin's docks hosted ships from all over the world and it was after all the capital of Kerala.

On leaving that morning I'd approached the station somewhat warily. I was told to pay on the train. With a porter I found the right coach and he drew the curtains to stop anyone else joining me. That was worth a nice tip. Eventually the ticket clerk arrived. I duly paid for my icily-cold splendour and managed to have the whole carriage to myself for the duration.

Once again I was arriving at an unknown railway station in the midday sun. If only I'd learnt all the words to the Noel Coward song, perhaps I wouldn't keep doing it.

On arrival, I found a porter, or rather he found me. I must have had that moderately frantic look of a mad dog and certainly three pieces of luggage should have generated a good tip. At this point I was still apprehensive as I was sure, as I'd been warned, that this man was going to rip me off for all the Buckley inheritance. My children would be left in poverty, my grandchildren might never visit Toys-R-Us with me again.

It turned out there was a scale of charges and even if he doubled it, it still wouldn't constitute the price of a 99 ice cream cone.

My hotel was at Kovalam. Directly on the beach and the gardens were so beautiful they had won awards. There were squirrels running up and down and jumping from tree to tree once they'd got a good swing going on the palm leaves. They differed from English squirrels in so much as they were still grey but had a black stripe up the middle of their back, about 1½ inches wide.

From my balcony I could see the waves crashing in and below me hammocks were slung beneath the palm trees. I ventured down to the beach twice. Our beach was called Samudra but just to the left was the main beach of Kovalam which seemed very busy but just with Indian people.

On our beach a young couple were paddling. I presumed they were honeymooners as they seemed completely engrossed in each other. The guide books had said the currents were dangerous at Kovalam. Did they mean like India was dangerous or was this based on scientific fact?

So I paddled gingerly, very gingerly, and hoped that three inches of seawater couldn't carry a sturdy piece of work like me off into the unknown. Despite the fact that I was in the water, the heat was unrelenting. I swiftly returned to the hotel and the swimming pool. I was being a bit of a wimp really but I've never claimed bravery in the face of unrelenting heat.

At the hotel that evening after dinner, one of the managers was paying me and my friends (more later) a lot of attention and hovering too much. At the end of the evening he said he'd bring a mosquito coil and show us how to light it later on. A knock at the door at 10.00pm and he said he'd already taken my friends theirs and he would now show me how to light mine. It took him quite a long time to get it going and judging by how close he got, he was used to sorting out more than mossie coils and I'm sure he's made some middle-aged women very happy. I think lighting a mosquito coil is a euphemism for something entirely different and the hovering in the garden is a way of sizing up the opportunities, and I seemed the only likely candidate.

I suppose it makes a change from "come up and see my etchings". He gave up gracefully when I got hold of his hand, shook it and still holding it propelled him towards the door and thanked him graciously. He must have heard me lock it quite noisily after him. I proceeded to put my cases in front of it. My night passed uneventfully, I do seem to get 'em . . . He wasn't creepy, just persistent.

I met some really nice people. They were South African Indians from Durban and they had the 15 day

Discover India Tour. Their 23 year old son was with them. He had just finished an engineering degree. Logi, the father, ran a security firm in Durban and I jokingly said that must be a growth industry and to my dismay it proved more than a joke. As we wandered the hotel grounds in the dark, casually chatting, it appeared they couldn't do that in their own garden in Durban. Far too dangerous. My worries about the dangers in India were dissolving as we spoke. Can't walk in your own garden in the evening, that's DANGER. That's no peace of mind.

We took a shared cab to the airport the next day and flew off in different directions, but not before I'd seen the camcorder the son was using. They're everywhere now but in 2000 it was the latest, tiny with a side picture to view what you were getting. I wasn't envious but I thought it must be nice to be able to afford such a gizmo.

As we left for the airport, the road on which we had approached the hotel was still under construction. There in the midday sun sat old men, women and children, all tapping away at large stones. They were making the hardcore as they went. Some had made shades from the coconut leaves. Further back towards the trees and what looked like woods, were makeshift houses. Coconut palms had been used to make these as well. One presumed that as the work progressed they moved as necessary. The able-bodied men seem to be making the roads themselves and driving HGVs etc. when needed.

The day before I left – well the only full day I had there – I decided I needed pens and paper. I ordered a taxi to take me downtown. I think, no, I know, something definitely got lost in translation because I just went

out of the hotel grounds, up the road, round a few corners and I was dropped off. Downtown it wasn't. It
just consisted of a row of cabins, kiosks, huts, the odd
cement building. As usual it was dusty and hot – it was
midday again. I wandered up and down. I got some
very strange looks. No-one in Valsad, Bombay or
Cochin had looked at me like this.

I was a real novelty, they'd got a live one. I don't
think any visitor had ever ventured to this particular
downtown of nine "businesses" on one side and a row
of rickstas on the other. The ricksta drivers looked like
they were taking bets on whether I managed to stay
the course for the full nine emporia. I felt obliged to
look at each one carefully and I tried to do business
with them all. A bottle of water here, a stale bun there,
a pen there, a tube of anti-viral cold sore cream here,
and finally a notepad. You may well wonder about the
cold sore cream, but I recognized it and knowing how
much I pay in the UK for said cream felt obliged to
buy two at 53p each. One tenth of the English price.
It's funny what you'll carry around with you if you
think you're saving money.

This was my first real time wandering on my own.
Daman was a dummy run, Cochin had been taxi door
to door, this was real life. I was feeling quite daring,
even light-headed with it, counting the seconds before
I could scurry back to the safety of my hotel. This
seemed like stepping into 5ft 6in of water when I was
only 5ft 4in.

The taxi had cost me 70 rupees. It was ordered by
the hotel and I checked the price before I left. So full
of bravado, knowing how much a taxi cost, I
approached the rickstas. In reply to my enquiry the
driver said 50 rupees. I said, "ok" and he turned to his
companion and said dismissively, "American" – Failed

at the first hurdle. I didn't barter, therefore I was made of money – there to be had. A punter, not a client of the Great India Tour Company. I suppose I had beginner tattooed across my forehead. From now on I'd get tougher.

At the airport on my arrival at Cochin I'd met a rep from London. She was mid-30's and Kovalam was just opening up with flights from London. That night friends had arranged for her to see the folk dancing which is famous in the region. She was there to research the area and report back.

The only other incident worth reporting from the hotel was when one day I chatted with the Hotel Manager. The general chat was about how industrious Indian people were and I thought that if they could provide the infrastructure and control corruption, no-one in the world could beat them. He said he was very flattered but that was just what a BA executive had said to him recently. I hurriedly checked it wasn't Bob Ayling – I did not want to be associated with anyone who changed the wingtips of our national carrier and then had to face the ignominy of changing them back at great cost. I did not want to be associated with failure of that magnitude. Hiring rickstas, yes possibly, corporate failure – never. By the way, the manager was sure I was a travel writer. Give me time, give me time.

CHAPTER FIFTEEN

Oh, yes, that elephant

You should see the security at Indian Airports. It was only internal flights as well. (This was before 9/11 but it appeared that India has had an internal flight high-jacked before). If they were this particular in NHS hospitals, more people would keep the right limbs instead of the clangers that do happen. How anyone can smuggle anything I've no idea. If they check your boarding card once, it is 20 times.

The car came to pick me up at Cochin airport to transfer me to Coconut Lagoon at Kumarakom. I didn't think it was too far away but there were a few main and many winding country roads.

As we were travelling along the main road we caught up and passed a ricksta. I stared in amazement and the driver said, "The nursery." I said, "The whole nursery?" There were many little faces peering at me at all angles. I can't hazard a guess at how many were in with their lunch boxes, but I've an idea they would have had to go round the back streets of Valsad or even across the rooftops to avoid detection.

There were feet sticking out sideways, with faces above them. I think the teacher had just shoved them in and hoped for the best. One thing is for certain, there would be no whiplash if they were in an accident, there wasn't enough room for that. My camera was packed away but I realized I was missing all sorts of things, so I scrabbled among my things till I found it. My driver dropped me for lunch at a nice hotel, waited and we were off again. He was English speaking and the car was air-conditioned. He informed me when I inquired about the communist state that it changed frequently. For a few years communism reigns, then the opposition take over for a few years, and then it changes back again. Tourism is coming in a big way there – the package tours start November 1st. London to Kovalam for the season. The people are so lovely and friendly. I hope they don't go like some of the Goan people.

When we arrived at the jetty to await the launch to take me to Coconut Lagoon, the driver said to me, "See the elephant." "Where?" says I, camera to hand. I couldn't see properly through my window, I hadn't a good view of anything really. When the driver pointed upwards, I realized it was the elephant which was blocking my view. Oh yes, that elephant. The one about 3 inches from my window. Dare I take a photo? Would the flash bother it? It was only recently I'd read of a girl being killed at an elephant show in Thailand, the organizers explaining that elephants were unpredictable as they were wild animals. How wild was this animal who had me at its mercy until my launch arrived?

Well, we looked each other in the eye and it allowed me to take its photo. A young boy, not realizing what the Thai organizers had said, was feeding it a coconut palm. His father was so thrilled that I took his son's picture that I reckon I could have been made an honorary aunt there and then.

The launch arrived just as darkness was falling and the 20 minutes or so it took to reach the island meant I arrived in darkness. The launch negotiated in off the lake through a narrow channel which brought us inside the reception building. I stepped onto dry land and was welcomed, as is normal, with leis and a coconut drink, much bowing on both sides, (hands pressed together), and I was escorted to my original, guaranteed authentic, Keralan boat house. Two floors all to myself, I was really rattling around.

As they were showing me round they opened a little door, about 4 feet high. I was ok but anyone tall would have trouble. You stepped down about 9 inches and got hit by about 85 degrees of heat. One loo, shower, wash basin and oh yes, a banana tree. Which meant you realized it hadn't got a roof. All a bit alarming. The stars twinkled down on you, you knew you'd stepped down, you were feeling slightly disorientated and you could hear voices passing by. They seemed to come from above. Could it be that the pathway outside looked down on your al fresco arrangements? Oh please, no. It would take until morning before I could be sure one way or the other. Perhaps this was communal living.

That night, about 3.00am. I plucked up courage, clambered out of my raised bed onto the little steps and gingerly made my way down the dark wooden stairs. With great difficulty, I pulled back the bolt and stepped down. This was no mean feat as the bolt was about 3 inches thick. The cicadas were going a bundle; a gecko was running freely and the mossies were circling. Whoever heard of applying repellent to go to the loo? I raced back indoors, shot the bolt and clambered all the way up the open plan staircase, up my little steps and into my bed. Authentic it may be, cosy it ain't. Some people though appeared to have bungalows which were more compact.

There was a little booklet, all made out of recycled paper in an impressive (ecologically) buff colour. The pen drawings were evocative and the prose was very good. No young students on the cheap had composed this. This looked like the work of the Professor Emeritus.

Coconut Lagoon, it states, is hidden away on the eastern shore of Lake Vembanad at the mouth of the Kavanar River. It is meant to give visitors an insight into Kuttanad life. It can be reached by boat and a ferry leaves from several mainland embarkation points at scheduled times.

The accommodation consists of Tharawads, the traditional wooden house. Some are recent builds but many are well over a century old and some actually date back to the early 1700's. They have been painstakingly dismantled from all over the region where because of high upkeep costs they had fallen into disrepair. Once at the lagoon they were assembled piece by piece in accordance with thachu shasthra, the ancient rules and rites of carpentry. Each ancient building is a veritable museum itself. Which is where the 3 inch wooden bolt comes in, I presume.

The grounds of the lagoon were interspersed with irrigation canals and the gardens were maintained around these. The whole area had a lush, ethereal quality to it. Terrified though I am of deep water, it fascinated me. I always gravitate towards water and am happiest by the side of it. Note I don't say "on it." Just beside it will do.

They sort of had a mission statement at the back of the booklet which states that the Casino Group of Hotels (they have the Lagoon, the one I was visiting next at Marari Beach, and I believe one in the rainforest called Spice Village or similar) are committed to preserving the social and cultural values of the local people whose land they share and whose talents they employ.

Since my visit in Autumn 2000 two holiday pro-grammes have visited the Lagoon and the rainforest location. And more than a few have taken a houseboat through the canals and across the lakes.

The language of Kerala is Malayalam, and Kuttanad in their language means land of the short people – so I'll be at home here. No, got that wrong. It's because the farmers were often seen walking knee-deep in the paddy fields.

Also since I visited Kerala, Paul McCartney has hon-eymooned there and it would apparently be the place to be seen. I can understand why. It was very peaceful and other-worldly. Life was not frenetic as in other parts of India and I should think the backwaters of Kerala could be where the expression "The backwaters of life," originated. If it didn't, it should have.

The backwaters had been here for at least 2 millen-nia. These were the very waterways that were the starting point for the transport of Southern Indian spices on their way to Europe and beyond.

They were formed by more than 40 rivers that flow from the Cardamom Hills in the Western Ghats to the Arabian Sea. The network of rivers, canals, lakes and estuaries runs parallel to the coast for about 100 miles.

The reception building is called a Nalukettu which is a four-cornered, open roofed structure. It was origi-nally a mansion belonging to a member of the Brahmin Caste constructed in 1860. Having passed through various hands it eventually was purchased in 1993 and using one of the few surviving craftsmen familiar with the traditional methods, it was recon-structed in its present location.

The restaurant, an Ettukettu, incorporates 2 atrium-like courtyards under a supported roof which allows any breeze to drift through. It formerly belonged to a prominent family in a nearby village.

My own house, other than the upstairs "grand lit" boudoir, had a living room, with fridge and desk areas. All the windows had intricate carvings and there were terracotta floors. Aigny and Jack were the woods used. The lampstands had been crafted from old wooden door hinges. Imagine the size of the door to which they were originally attatched. Upstairs you had views over the lake and the windows were all around on two of the sides, about 2 foot high. It took ages drawing all the curtains. I was still moderately nervous because there was this unknown danger. I suppose the only real problem with the open plan bathroom was because I was on my own. Romantically, showering à deux under the stars probably can't be beaten.

The booklet recommends, and I can second that, the free-form pool. It was elevated to give a lake view, which includes for those who swim early evening, the sound of classical Indian music drifting across from the Garden Café. Bamboo fishing poles are available from the swimming pool attendant and the Chef promises to cook anything, within reason, the angler catches. I hasten to add, the catches are meant to come from the lake and canals, not the pool.

In the cautions at the back of the book, one of the warnings is not to attempt to climb any of the coconut trees and pick coconuts on your own. The trees are higher than you think. Does that mean they do escorted climbing and picking? I'll pass on that. Or could they have had British lager louts?

It's so ecological round there that they purify their

own water – surely a first in India, and treat and modify their waste products for use on the gardens. Washing is sent to the mainland.

It was ecological, but strange as it might seem, I was now to check out the boutique. It might be backwoods stuff, but only so far. Remember, this is India and Indians never miss a chance to make a sale.

I hadn't noticed any white British. There were Swiss, English Indians (ex East Africa). Belgians, Americans and Germans all in the swimming pool at once. There was also a famous middle-aged Hindu singer and his girlfriend, very beautiful, half his age.

Whilst waiting for the launch to collect me when I first arrived, I saw some houseboats. They looked incredibly romantic and I got talking to the owner. He did a good sales job showing me round two of them. Very luxurious, he charged $300 per night for two double-bedded rooms, bathroom, sitting room, library, all food and drink, sun deck and then kitchen at the stern. Given the heat and the mossies plus the fact that I'd paid for my nights at the Lagoon I resisted an overnight stay. He said he'd do a deal for a day trip. Isn't that what people who go to Margate do? He offered it for about £30.00. I decided it was my Christmas present to myself and booked it.

So there I was the next day waiting for my 63 foot houseboat to collect me and take me through this fascinating dream-like world. I was to have my own Chef and 2 boatmen. I'd seen them yesterday and they were hunks. The boat was fitted out in mahogany and rosewood.

We set off, punting by pole. We passed a man up to his lower chest in water. He seemed to be treading water. I asked what he was doing. Apparently this was how he got the mussel shells from the bottom of the lake to provide lime. Another alternative to this explanation was to trap a fish called a pearlspot.

If I hadn't already booked this I would possibly have considered going in one of the hotel canoes for a few hours near the lagoon.

When I got on board I was greeted warmly and taken on a conducted tour of my new *empire*-for-a-day. They wanted to show me the kitchen but I told them I wasn't interested. They didn't understand, they thought all women were interested in the kitchen, well not this one, at least not in this heat.

50,000 people live on the backwaters and it would seem kick one and they all limp. It appeared the little boy I photographed with the elephant was the nephew of the main boatman. So of course I was flavour of the month. Saying that, I'm sure they treated everyone in the same wonderful, friendly way.

We reached the shore at the other side of the lake and there we picked up our ice-box. I was then shown 3 different types of fish – packed in ice, sterilized ice I hoped, but it didn't matter, the fish would be cooked. Now I only eat dark fish and couldn't quite make myself understood on this one. For people who live, eat and drink fish this was probably a hard one. I chose the one I hoped would taste "dark." I then had to choose lunchtime and opted for 2.00pm.

When lunch did arrive they'd cooked some prawns for me as well but I couldn't eat everything – there was enough for 4 people. The Chef looked quite disappointed, coupled with not being interested in his kitchen, I'm sure I'm not on his Christmas card list this year. Then again, this just could have been some acting practised over the years which really meant, "Goody, more for us."

In the fruit bowl in the stateroom – am I getting a

little too grand do you think? – there had been a pineapple about 15 inches long. This disappeared and then reappeared, dissected and trimmed to perfection. Despite its size I finished the lot. I was also being offered beers and cokes. They seemed surprised I didn't want either but I succumbed to coke in the end, along with the bottled water, dehydration could not set in.

I could have had a lie down in the big green bed. I declined. It was enclosed and sported just a static small fan on the headboard. Thank goodness I hadn't chosen to spend the night. Air-conditioning to some meant different things. I now see it can mean anything from the desk-model fan over the bed, ceiling fans through to air conditioning units, some smelly, some noisy, some smelly and noisy and very rarely, some ok.

The main boatmen spoke excellent English and whenever I asked questions did his best to answer me. He showed me a book in the library and recommended I read it as it was by a famous Indian writer, R. S. Narayan. The book was not too thick so I started it and managed to finish whilst sunbathing. It threw another angle of Indian life into perspective with interesting vignettes of the perplexities of human nature.

Once we got going and they found out I wanted to sunbathe, out came a white cotton sheet and it was draped and folded over the bow. On the one I'd been shown at the jetty, it had been a pink silk sheet. A bolster was put at either end and a feeling of last of the great moghuls or peel me another grape Caesar began to take over. It seemed hedonistic. It was hedonistic – but for one day and my Christmas present to myself – it was ok. A wooden table with short curved legs was placed on the sheet and my drink and fruit on that. I could learn to live like this.

With cool box on board we'd set off down the lake and it took a couple of hours to get all the way down. After punting for a short while, an outboard motor finally took over. We weren't going slowly. I've still no idea how big the lake is, but I can report it was full of the floating blue water hyacinths which seems to proliferate on many waterways in the East.

We passed many boats plying their trade, some fishing, some transporting. The houseboats, until the advent of the tarmacadam road and the HGVs, were the normal transport between the interior and the coast. Their look owes something to the Chinese influence of trading patterns.

Locals use a variety of boats. Their version of the houseboat no longer requires living accommodation. It usually just has a curved hood about 6 feet long halfway along and is still used for transporting. A Kettuvallam (sewn canoe) is often laden with all manner of things. I don't think they transfer small loads. It's full or it doesn't go. Sometimes these canoes are traders selling their wares to the community, other times it's the water HGV.

People are often at the water's edge. Some women were washing clothes, some themselves. You are not meant to stare if they are washing themselves as this is like somebody opening your bathroom door and looking in. It's just not done. It's riverside etiquette. Many children were swimming and wherever we went everyone waved. They seemed so open and friendly. There were little churches all over the place and I thought there must be one for every village. Now and again you could see a school. Neat little bungalows were perched on narrow strips of grass, surrounded by irrigation canals. Children, so young, played near the water and one presumed they'd had swimming lessons before they left the womb, either that or their mothers weren't easily stressed.

A very long canoe went by with a crowd of people on board. This must have been the local ferry. Coconut leaves and branches are regularly transported. As with many Eastern nations, the coconut is one of the major sources for income and energy for use in houses and commerce.

As I watched and passed the bungalows, I noticed chicks and ducks running all over. The odd cow grazed, there were many pigs and goats. This was the streets of Valsad with more greenery. Valsad with irrigation channels. Churches instead of temples. It was so verdant as to be a different country from the North near Bombay.

The side flaps (made of coconut reeds) could be flipped open to give a breeze through the entire houseboat. It gave a winged look to it. Power was supplied by solar panels – but you didn't notice them.

I enjoyed the trip better when we were near the lakeside and up the narrow canals where I could see life happening. I had to ask to go there. It seemed to be the big trip was across the lake but I like to putter between banks, trees and under bridges. The broad expanse, except at dawn or sunset is not my favourite.

I returned back just at dusk to see the Hindu singer and his girlfriend and assorted visitors just getting out of the hotel boat where they'd been on an hour's trip. I remember thinking cheapskate about him, but then I didn't know the whole story.

CHAPTER SIXTEEN

The Hindu film star

During the general chat on the houseboat, religion came up and I mentioned I was a Catholic and surprised to find my religion in India so prolific. The boatman suggested if I wanted to go to Mass on Sunday, one of the reception staff would take me. He introduced me to him and I arranged to be at reception at 10.00am.

It was very hot, as usual and we set off on the hotel's ferry. At this stage, I had no idea geographically where I was. For all I knew I could be miles from civilisation. After about 10 minutes we got off at a designated stop by a bridge.

We climbed some steps and I was amazed to see a road with cars passing by. The young man escorting me said we had to go by bus, did I mind? I assured him it was fine. I'd only have to hitchhike and travel on an HGV and I'd have done every form of transport on the sub-continent. I'll make a backpacker yet.

Whilst we waited he got me another bottle of water, wouldn't take any money for it, nor for the bus fare. He said he was honoured.

I got very many curious looks when I entered the bus. I'm positive they'd probably never had a European on one round there before. It wasn't very far along the dusty road and we dismounted from the air-cooled bus to intense heat.

We turned up a path, a road it was, but that dignified it with formality. It was about 10ft wide, dusty as usual with ditches on either side. I could see the church, it wasn't too far, but it felt like a long way in the heat.

My escort motioned to me to take off my sandals and pointed to one side of the church, he went round the other. He told me to go under a ceiling fan but I didn't feel I could push my way towards one. Ladies on the left, men on the right.

The church was dramatic, and the altar was filled with a myriad of coloured, artificial flowers. I realized all the women had their heads covered by their saris or veils and of course I was bareheaded. I was wearing a cotton, sleeveless top, a short-sleeved cotton shirt, unbuttoned and a skirt. As it came up to communion, I started to struggle out of my shirt, no mean feat, allowing the ceiling fans were way beyond me. I pulled the sleeves in and tried to fold in the collar as I raised it over my head. I'm not sure it worked, but I like to follow the local custom, I didn't want to offend anyone. When the blessing was done the blessing was passed from the altar boy along each row.

It was very like Catholicism in the UK 1950s. The priest faced the altar away from the congregation and I've a rough idea that the shock waves would reverberate to Portugal if it was mooted that there could be altar girls as well as altar boys in Kerala, as in the UK.

I've now heard sermons in 17 different languages on my travels. In Wales I regularly go to the Welsh language mass and there's another conducted totally in Polish not very far away, work that one out . . .

I got my camera out to take a picture of the ornate and colourful altar after the priest had left. As he exited stage right, the curtains came down as though triggered by a wire as he disappeared. Either that or someone had spotted the tourist's camera and they were having none of that. The curtains were blood red satin and descended as dramatically as a fire curtain in the theatre. I was quite stunned. Ah well, back to the dirt road.

I met my escort outside. He asked did I enjoy it. Other questions he asked were curiosity about my religion in the UK. He found it hard to believe it was the same. Did we adore the Mother Mary? I assured him we did and he seemed satisfied. It made a change to be on the end of the questions instead of the other way round.

I was leaving that day and at reception I met the girlfriend of the Hindu singer. Boy how I'd got that wrong. I was told he was a singer by a waiter because in the restaurant some schoolchildren were getting his autograph and taking his picture.

On talking to her, I found out she was the Hindu singer, he was the Hindu film star. They'd been staying in a secluded bungalow with its own swimming pool – so you see he wasn't such a cheapskate after all, but what do I know?

One thing I do know is that she and I were getting on great. I'd paid my bill, he was paying theirs and then joined us. We were all on the launch back to the mainland. We carried on chatting as we waited. I got their picture for Dipti's children and then she said we should all have one together. So there we are on the launch – friends for life. Well, actually we could have been. He gave me his card and said when I came through Bombay on my way back to give him a ring. He put his mobile number on it as well. They both wanted to show me round Bombay. Could I get to go to Bollywood? Then again he may have heard about my TV appearance and he wanted to give me a part in his next film as an Indian dancer.

We arrived at the mainland and I was picked up by my driver. Wonderful. I like this sort of life. What danger?

Back on the main road we passed a line of working elephants, hauling logs and carrying things. A man sat astride each one. There was a thick chain around the animal which sat just behind its front legs. The man sat between this and a thick rope, doubled, round its neck. There was no official seat, so a cloth was underneath him and his feet were under the neck rope for balance. He had a thin twig in his hand. This twig, given its circumference, would have felt to an elephant as a fly landing on us. It must only have been used for guidance. The elephants themselves had healthy-looking hides and unlike some creatures in foreign countries did not appear malnourished.

Other elephants I saw as we passed back and forward between the main road and our route were working or sometimes just standing around. The work seemed to consist of moving heavy stuff. One was outside a rather elaborate and colourful entrance to a temple. It seemed to be taking it easy and just grazing. I wondered if it was a pet. Can you have full-sized pet elephants?

I've read that the Indian elephant is under threat and Kerala is one of the few places left in India with them. They've also got tigers but I gave them a miss. William Blake's, "Tiger, tiger, burning bright," coupled with an old Sabu film has put me right off them for life.

A big celebration in April/May has 30 caparisoned elephants. That is, done up in gold finery, in fact, ablaze with the amount of gold, walking in a single line 30 wide. There are riders standing on each one with what appear to be ostrich-type balls of feathers in each hand. A traditional Indian sun parasol in red, trimmed with gold is over them. There seems to be one animal, the central star of the show, with a blue parasol, arrayed in a gold shield trimmed with flowers. The throbbing beat of Chendamelam, (Keralan music) accompanies them. Quite a spectacle. Oh yes, and there are fireworks.

Back at the lagoon there was a bird sanctuary on the southern bank of the Kavanar River. Now these didn't mean as much to me as they would to Bill Oddie or any twitcher worth his name, but there were darters, bitterns, Brahminy kites, marsh harriers and many herons and egrets. Yes, but were there any robins?

The men in Kerala and I believe in other parts of the south wear skirts or dhotis, usually in Madras cotton. (Madras is on the other coast if you draw a straight line across.) Mahatma Gandhi never made this sort of garment look sexy but believe me they are. They're up, they're down and just like the Grand Old Duke of York, they're often halfway up. Half the day is spent adjusting them. It's a way of life. If you have to do anything other than walk it necessitates plucking the corners and hoisting the skirt up, folding and tucking as you go. It takes seconds. If they ever wear trousers (in reception they do) – they must be forever hitching them up). You know when a smoker gives up, well when my husband did he always said that he didn't know what to do with his hands. Well, having a Keralan skirt would have cured that. If I'd known about it, I'd have been investing in a piece of Madras cotton long ago.

In most countries the south is the hottest region, well here in India, although not very cool, the south is cooler than the north. Delhi and Rajasthan were the highest at that time with 38° and of course that was where I was going. Even Katmandu in Nepal was 28°. I thought winter had begun there and I would have to buy a coat for the Himalayas but it appeared not. At my hotel on Indian Christmas Day I should have a view of the third highest mountain in the world. In Kerala it was a rather parky 30 degrees.

Back to the backwaters.

Eventually we arrived at my new hotel. I was completely at a loss due to the rabbit warren of lanes we had traversed to know in which direction we had come. It was called Marari Beach but this confused me even more as I thought I was inland somewhere. Was it a beach at a lake?

The driver would collect me after a couple of days to take me to the airport at Cochin. Having poured over a map of India and perused, for many hours, the airline schedules, I had decided to save time by getting a flight from Cochin to Madras now called Chenai and catching another flight the same day to Calcutta. I should overnight in Calcutta. Then up to the Himalayas. Just writing it sounded wonderful.

As I'd travelled in Kerala, I'd had various taxis and in one there was the usual rosary beads hanging down, coupled with a picture of the Sacred Heart. Another had the Holy Family with flashing lights round them. In Bombay they had Hindu gods similarly decorated. Did it mean taxis were dangerous – had I solved my mystery danger? – and the drivers needed all the help they could get? The HGVs were decorated ostentatiously outside once again with whichever deity was worshipped by the driver. So you get Christian HGVs, Buddhist HGVs, Hindu, Sikh and Muslim HGVs. They might say the equivalent to John Smith & Son, Builders and Joiners on the side, but it was the religion they were proclaiming which was just as important.

So, as I said, I arrived at Marari Beach. We entered in the middle of a small town, perhaps large village, then down a long driveway after the gates had been opened. The grounds were immaculate. This was a sister hotel to Coconut Lagoon and in keeping with this fine tradition, I was escorted to a beautiful, thatched bungalow with its own open plan bathroom. But this one was different. Instead of a banana tree I had a papaya, which were unfortunately under-ripe.

My bungalow was opposite my own pond complete with ducks and other wildlife, not too far from reception. The bathroom as I saw it in daylight presented more problems than the last. It had its own door which led outside to the garden. I noticed that outside the bungalow, there was a box against one of the walls about 3 feet high by 12 inches wide which I supposed housed the electrics. Even I could climb onto this ledge and from there it was another 2ft to a ledge over my personal bathroom wall. Was this the danger? How did the family back in Valsad know about this then?

The bungalow itself was spacious but cosy at the same time. In fact if I could forget the bathroom I would feel a lot more secure than my vast house at Coconut Lagoon.

As I wandered around the grounds, I could hear the water crashing in. Did lakes have crashing waves? That must be some breeze. I made my way towards it, past a thatched bar which did beach food. I emerged from the trees along the path, waves about 3ft high were pounding the beach. If this were a lake, they'd made a good job getting all the sand there.

There was a guard patrolling. I now realized that the hotel grounds and my ledge just below my bathroom wall were open to the main beach. Slow though I was – I think I was tired with all the travelling – it was dawning on me that this was the main beach for the town and I was on the Arabian Sea coastline again.

Now I can follow a map anywhere, sideways, upside down, but it only took a few turns of a taxi down a few country lanes to disorientate me so I'd never be able to pin the tail on the donkey with or without a blindfold.

When I finally left Marari, I was speaking to one of the receptionists, a very nice, pretty girl with excellent English. She'd probably attended an English medium school. She said when the hotel was being finished and the staff accommodation wasn't ready she'd been assigned to a bungalow. Like me, she felt very vulnerable with the bathroom, the ledge and the outside door. Although the hotel has been there a bit, I feel eventually this may become a security problem, although they have many security guards patrolling the grounds.

Like at the lagoon, everything was beautifully done. It was well run and there was an Ayurvedic Centre which I'd just booked. I'd used one in Samudra and the massage was done in such a way and with so many oils I nearly slithered off the table. Two people massage simultaneously from top to bottom in a quite fast rhythmic motion. There is a 2½ inch lip round the sides of the plastic table, without which you'd be launched in your teenie-weenie paper knickers onto the unsuspecting world outside the clinic as you slithered past. You probably wouldn't stop till you reached the sea in whichever direction it was. Still my skin felt wonderful afterwards.

I visited the beach again, stopping for a drink and lunch (a toastie) at the bar among the trees. A young Australian was working there. We chatted for a bit, he was going round the world but he still struggled to understand the toastie machine. Someone after my own heart.

I met some Indians from Cochin. Well travelled, well educated, a man, his wife, her sister and family. They said I was seeing more of India than they had. This shouldn't surprise me as there are possibly some tourists visiting the UK who have seen more of that than I have.

There were fishing boats on the beach which shelved, evenly, but quite quickly. They were launched with the maximum of manual labour. They had a look of a Viking longboat and the men (skirts hoisted) rocked and pushed them until the sea took over. This was being done towards dusk, so I presumed they'd be night fishing. About 20 men jump aboard as it slithered into the sea.

To the side of the path leading from the hotel were palm trees and wicker-sunshades over the loungers. There were several circular thatched, open diners. As the season was just starting no-one seemed to be manning them. Here and there, there were hammocks slung between the coconut palms. I would not try out one of these because (1) I'm not dexterous enough and (2) I am no judge as to if the coconuts could be ready to fall and concuss me or worse.

In the pool I had been chatting to many different nationalities. There were many French and Swiss there. They were trading with the Indians in coir. This was the major source for them and their families seemed to have joined them for a holiday. I was left wondering how I could get on this gravy train and be of use to the UK coir industry. Were we utilising all our chances on the sub-continent? Could I facilitate anything by lounging by the pool and networking? Possibly not, I usually chose the temperature I worked in.

CHAPTER SEVENTEEN

Enough oil to launch the next P&O liner

As I was dining that evening at dinner, the Maître d' told me he had a phone call for me and gave me a mobile phone. Now I hate them (it means people can get hold of me) and I didn't know all the etiquette then. I was also rather embarrassed and instead of taking myself off to a quiet corner, and I didn't know where that was yet, I shouted into it at my table. I had to shout because I couldn't hear what this strange man was saying. It appeared he was the agent in Delhi who was hoping to arrange my Rajasthan tour. He confirmed the first two nights in the Himalayas and he was telling me who, what and why.

Rather sheepishly, I removed my finger from my ear and handed the phone back. People seemed to be ok and no-one was harrumphing or tutting. There were sympathetic smiles. No harm done to any entente cordiale. On my way to dinner I passed the amphitheatre in which a beautiful, young girl was singing hauntingly in the dark, just her floodlit on the stage. She was made up dramatically in the Keralan way. It was a bit like the over emphasis when making up opera stars. Her voice echoed through the night and at the end the audience seated on their white plastic patio chairs, clapped enthusiastically. There were many children among them. I wished I'd made the effort and arrived for the start. She gave an encore and it was over. Her actions were melodramatic and deliberate as this was Kerala's version of Western opera.

In the restaurant each night a different type of musical entertainment was provided. One night, classical Indian, another a pop band playing golden oldies, another night, Indian pop. Heavily accented, "Save the last dance for me," or "Are you lonesome tonight?" could only work in this setting.

Once again I duly presented myself at the Ayurvedic Centre. The Ayurvedic principles developed in Kerala thousands of years ago and it is considered the world centre for the treatment. The doctor explained to me that I wasn't going to be there long enough to make a difference. People usually came for at least a week. They seemed to come mainly from Switzerland, some from Germany, but also many UK Indians. Drat, I suppose I'll just have to slither around again, restrained by a 2 ½ inch lip and suffer a massage. Lead me to it.

This time two giggling ladies, quite mature, were going to do the massage. I looked around for the paper knickers. Peals of laughter. There was going to be no such thing. They apparently were for wimps or for hotels catering for tourists' sensibilities. This was a serious Ayurvedic centre. And we were off. To say it was vigorous was an understatement of mammoth proportions. At least if I left the table here, I stood a chance of landing in either my duck pond or the swimming pool. If the worst happened and I shot too far, too fast, perhaps I could give the boys a help launching their boat on the beach. Could be I'd unravel a few Madras skirts as I went.

They were nice thoughts as I was abrazed by two mistresses of the art. As they worked, they chatted to each other, punctuated by a laugh or giggle on a regular basis. When you're at your most vulnerable, it does-n't do to hear giggling. Were they laughing about something their little boy said, or was it more proba-ble, wondering how many cream cakes it took to achieve my Venus de Milo figure? Well, I wasn't telling them. They indicated by sign language for me to turn over. Were they mad? It was taking me all my time to maintain my equilibrium on my back. The table was only about 24 inches wide, the amount of oil running down it could provide free running for the next P&O liner at its launch.

Gingerly I edged side on and then as I put my hand down to lever over, I slipped. There was a sound of wet fish landing on a slab – quite a big fish, in fact it could be said that this one would break all records. Relief though, I was over and clinging on to the rim for dear life as the massage started again. Despite the strength of the massage, it was very relaxing, soporific even. As it finished, I was signed again to get down. I opted for the line of least resistance and slid down to the end and off. I was then rubbed down to remove excess oil. I padded as carefully as I could to the changing room. As my clothes clung lovingly to my body, I slithered back to my bungalow.

Chatting later in the day to some local Indians I found that they were paying a lot less than me for their rooms (what's new?). It was costing me £25 per night more. I tackled my agent about this and he told me he hadn't the clout to obtain a larger discount. I accepted it, after all I was being taken door to door in case the danger got me.

I wonder how the woman and the peacock were going on. Could it be an urban Indian myth?

The next morning my private taxi arrived again to

escort me to Cochin airport. By the end of the day I would have flown across the southern part of India and then gone north almost to the Himalayas. There wouldn't be much of India left north of me.

A short flight brought me to Madras, I'd got 5 hours before my next so I hired a ricksta, negotiated a rate for my sightseeing, took my camera and a spare film and set off.

The driver's English was so-so. He took me downtown Madras (Chenai) past very exotic looking temples. The carvings were spectacular. This was a part of the country which has brought carving and story telling on the walls of the buildings to an artform of the most magnificent splendour.

Due to someone loading the camera incorrectly – and I admit, I am on my own, – none of this was filmed. I shot film in parks, by great temples, at the shore. Out of 32 films, this and another were the only ones which didn't make it.

After a while I asked the driver to go for lunch. I wanted 4 Star as I had with my private taxi – he had understood and he found a large hotel – but this driver had his own ideas. After a short while we turned into a street which looked like a bazaar. There was just enough room for our ricksta to get through. Shops and businesses crammed every part as it came to a T-junction. The streets were jam-packed with bodies. There seemed to be ricksta parking to the left, and my driver pulled in beside the others.

I was now in the middle of a melee, the only white face for miles. My smiling driver pointed to a restaurant – quite large, but 4 Star it wasn't. I'd be surprised if it registered on the greasy spoon scale. Within two and a half hours I'd gone from being over-protected with my private taxi to no idea where I was, who the driver was, or if I could trust him. In fact, could I trust anyone round there? Was the restaurant safe, would my Harrod's bags still be there when I returned, would my ricksta even be there? If that happened what would I do?

By now it was just leaving midday, how do I did it? Bugger it, I was up to my eyes in it now. I might as well be full with some food if I'd to tackle anything untoward. I realize now how I'd ended up there. I have found that Indians even when they understand you, do what they want. If they think something is better for you, then that's what you get. This chap thought I'd be better off saving money at this restaurant, so that's where we went. Sometimes it's because it's better for them and then you get stonewalled. I haven't worked out whether it's because I'm a woman, a foreigner or both.

Tentatively I entered the restaurant. All eyes turned towards me. The tables were fixed with benches on either side. A bit like the Wimpy bars in the 50's and 60's. The Manager, a very tall man, came towards me. His English was quite good and he seated me.

I could see from the huge black boards over the kitchen it was a vegetarian restaurant. Not at all unusual in India. I chose what I knew to be a mild potato curry with naan bread. The Manager brought me an ice cream to finish. I idly wondered where it had been prepared. Who cared? My ricksta might not be outside when I emerged. I had bigger worries.

The other diners were mixed. Many dining together, some families, including Grandma. None were particularly well dressed. This was day-to-day India in a run down part of town.

I chatted to the Manager as I paid. Although the

restaurant/café was down market to say the least – my meal cost about £1.00 + coke – he was well educated and naturally extremely polite. We shook hands and I left.

As the heat hit me, I realized not only could I not remember what my driver looked like, but I didn't even remember to note the ricksta number. I fixed a confident smile on my face and glanced around casually. I felt a wide eyed look would attract the wrong sort of attention. I could hardly expect to blend in as I conducted my eye search.

Just as the heat began to drain me – I felt like a battery whose life was running out fast – a man approached me. I thought I recognized him – I hope I did, because I was allowing him to guide me to a ricksta – and there safe and sound were my Harrod's bags. This must be my driver. It's not easy when you've only seen the back of his head and now and again the face in profile.

This time we were visiting the shore. We drove along the road which ran parallel with the sands. The breakers were quite strong and Indian families were on the beach. There were many fishing boats and on the other side of the road were makeshift homes, some more permanent than others. Goats, pigs, hens, dogs and cows were ever present. Very young children wandered around backwards and forwards in the road. No-one seemed to think that, at 15 months old, they were stupid enough to go in the water or disappear up the road. They were probably right.

At one point the houses stopped and stalls appeared. They sold shells, necklaces, drinks and knick-knacks. I strolled around among them but didn't buy. I'd have felt worse just selecting one or two people when they all were obviously desperate for business. I returned to my ricksta.

I was delivered back to the airport in good time. I paid the agreed fee and tip and we parted friends. I'd forgiven him for lunch, it wasn't anywhere near as bad as I'd expected. If I became ill, chances are I would change my mind. I'm easily swayed like that.

I flew into Calcutta and by then it was nearly dark. Was this where the danger was? That question would be answered at a later date, and although this time I was not sure, the second time I was.

I was staying at an airport hotel, I'd been reunited with my luggage as The Great India Tour Co. had looked after it for me when I only took beach things to Kerala. I definitely needed a taxi. I ordered one as I left the building and shared it with an Israeli girl who was travelling India, we'd met at departure at Cochin airport .

She said she couldn't afford where I was staying, so she'd go to a hostel, but instead of the driver dropping me off first as we passed my hotel, we travelled to another down market area and now it was completely dark.

I looked forlornly as we passed my hotel. He might be working on the principle that I would be able to afford the full fare and the girl might not as she was budgeting.

We stopped in an alleyway just big enough to take the taxi. People, all nationalities, were pushing past on either side and the taxi rocked with the force. The girl went into the hostel and the driver accompanied her as he'd recommended it. He was gone about 20 minutes. It felt like 3 months and I was checking out everyone as they passed. I was nervous, a bit jittery as this could be what they've been talking about.

Sweet relief swept over me as he returned and we progressed to my hotel. I thanked him, paid him and checked in. As I was coming back that way I arranged for my suitcase to be left with the concierge. I changed everything over and left the beach things in Calcutta. I was off early the next day for the Himalayas. Life was good. I was becoming intrepid – I think?

I got out my Lonely Planet Guide and studied it intently. It informed me that I would be able to get a jeep to take me up the Himalayas. A warm, relaxed glow came over as I was reading, and a thought struck me. Just to the right was my bathroom and for the first time in 5 days I realized I would be able to use a loo where you weren't worried who was going to appear over the wall. And there's something I never thought I'd ever write.

CHAPTER EIGHTEEN

Sold to the highest bidder

From Calcutta I caught the midday plane to Bagdogra airport. Planes go three times a week, so the return has to be well-planned or you're stuck there and your schedule is all to pot.

I kept reading my Lonely Planet Guide on the plane but still wasn't sure how I got to Siliguri for the jeep.

As we waited for the plane at Calcutta I saw all these middle-aged people. Middle England really, on the move. They were smartly dressed, with a leaning towards more women than men. I saw one woman writing in her diary. My immediate thought was that they were with Cox and Kings.

Well, surprise, surprise, they were. The luggage labels proudly proclaimed their origin. I wondered if I'd ever see them again.

By this time, I was only sporting my two Harrods bags and to save weight I'd cut off the two little Harrod's doormen in their green livery. They were solid, heavy, little things. My shoes were down to the sandals I was wearing plus one pair of evening sandals. This was fantastically good for me as I usually travelled with a minimum of six pairs.

I only had two or three changes of clothes. I was resigned to buying warmer if the Himalayas demanded it.

The plane was only small, 66 seater I think and it was full. We landed almost as soon as we set off, so once again I was arriving full in the midday sun.

As I left the plane, I saw the Cox and Kings' lot

milling around, not for them the vagaries of getting to the jeep stand. They were probably excited but nothing could have topped the way I felt. Off into the unknown and no-one (family, friends etc.) really knew where I was going – then again, I'd only a rough idea. My hotel was 4½ hours away. I'd booked it to be certain of somewhere to stay for Diwali.

Inside the airport lounge, a small affair, there was a desk saying pre-paid taxis. This seemed a good idea. Money handed over, I was given a piece of paper with a vehicle registration number on it. I emerged blinking into blinding sunshine and a sea of faces, clutching 2 bags and a bit of paper.

At the doorway, someone grabbed the paper and called out I don't know what. A man climbed forward and claimed me. This was my taxi I presumed or I'd just been sold to the highest bidder as I had my own teeth and looked like I had a good few years work left in me.

So off I went and sure enough the number on my paper corresponded with his taxi. Following the instructions in my guide book, I just said, "Jeep stand, Siliguri please", and hoped that was enough. I was pleasantly surprised when, within half an hour, I was dropped at the stand. To get there we'd ploughed through a bizarre type of traffic jam, camels, cycloshaws (a bike with cyclist and single seat for passenger), scooters, cars and the usual Cadbury's assortment of animals. It was like Spaghetti Junction on speed.

I thanked the taxi driver and took hold of my bags. The queue had about eight in it. All men of course. I think I was the only European in town – well, at least, in view.

As soon as I got a bit nearer in the queue, I was skipped. Had they not heard of queueing or standing in line? But why should I expect people in another very foreign country to abide by my rules? So, working on the principal of, "If you can't beat 'em etc," I started to elbow my way to the front. This passed without a hitch, my elbows must have indicated my determination. As I hit the front I said to the man in the little wooden stand, as per the guide book, that I wanted to share a jeep to Darjeeling. As he charged me the princely sum of 80p, even then I didn't twig. There was a sign saying luggage carried at owner's risk. I remember thinking if I lost it Amex would have to kit me out again. Mind you, I still hadn't assessed the risk, I was just pleased as punch at my success at the jeep stand.

How much of a success this was became apparent as I was handed a piece of paper in exchange for my money with a registration number on it. As I turned away from the stand I was waiting for someone within this seething mass of humanity to grab my paper and organize it for me. No-one did.

So in the midday heat I looked at the number and was faced with a plethora of jeeps. All were white and so far none of the numbers corresponded to mine. As I panned round eventually my eyes lit on a tired, dirty-looking jeep with canvas sides. Yep, that was mine.

In the Lonely Planet I'd got the idea that there would be four of us in the jeep. I can't blame Lonely Planet but that was what I thought. That's roughly how many they take in the UK. I hadn't forgotten I was in India, but for some reason jeep meant Western civilisation and four was a nice number.

There were many beggars about but to give them their due they didn't bother me until I was seated. I was just climbing into the spare seat in my jeep – not easy with my short legs and two bags when someone asked me what number my seat was. I stopped mid-way, one leg in and one still dangling. I balanced precariously, clinging on to the back of the seat to my left. Seat number? This wasn't a jumbo jet, it wasn't even a train, coach or mini-bus. For heaven's sake, it was a jeep, and a ramshackle one at that.

It turned out that mine was number 12 and I was "round the back". One of my bags was taken and thrown up between the roof rack and I had to climb up – with a friendly hoist from inside over the spare type – I've already got one of those – and I was in. My number seemed to be the first seat nearest the front on the left.

As I sat waiting for the off, the thought occurred to me that somewhere in the background in Siliguri, a group of Cox and Kings' tourists were being met by sanitized jeeps and whisked off to their holiday hide-away. They might be thrilled but they wouldn't be half as exhilarated as I was as I waited for the driver. The fact that someone else was organizing your luggage and itinerary and you weren't in charge of your own destiny must dampen the spirits somewhat. I almost felt like a backpacker. I'd missed my backpacking years having children – this was my time.

The guide book said the jeep trip was hair-raising, even death-defying, but worth it for the views. Alternatively you could take the train, but that was 8 hours. Much as I love trains, that seemed excessive and the words hair-raising raised just enough hairs to tempt me. If they'd also described fording rivers in the jeep, there would have been no contest. As it was, I did consider the train but only for about 5 minutes. Thoughts of eight hours avoiding Indian train toilets also didn't help the decision in the train's favour.

As we set off I noticed the driver was about 18. Did this bode well or not? In the UK this would be enough to have everyone baling out PDQ. Perhaps no-one past the age of 21 could handle all the corners, arthritis would have set in by then with overuse.

Including the driver there were four in the front, four on the 2nd row and then at the back, sideways on, there was myself and one guy and three others facing us. One or two people were standing on the spare tyre.

We stopped for petrol and this was where the real beggars were. As keen as any I've seen. As we left, I noticed we'd acquired more passengers, so as we drove along the flat before the long ascent, there were 18 aboard. Two were on the luggage and three on the back bumper and tyre. The other 13 were inside. It makes me wonder where I got the idea from of about 4 to a jeep. The price should have given it away.

Still on the flat, a few miles out of town, there was a shout. One poor devil at the back had fallen off and all we could see was half of his face, his eyes wide with alarm and the fingers of his hands as he clung on.

The driver stopped, but didn't turn the engine off. There was a lot of Nepalese chatter – but I don't think suing the arse off the jeep company came into it – so not the UK then – and eventually the guy limped off across the road. Apparently his foot had gone under the wheel.

On writing home to my family I had wondered if the poor blighter should have had the seat next to me and couldn't do so because of my big rear. My guilt was assuaged later on by a guide who said the man had been travelling for free – as I presumed so were those guarding my luggage as I'd come to think of them. I hoped they were guarding it, as the other thought was that they could be rifling through it and this was the danger everyone had been warning me about.

Inside the jeep there was absolutely no talking among the twelve passengers and driver. I think we were all concentrating too much on making sure we made all the corners. To say it was switchback was putting it mildly; but it wasn't as bad as Bombay – Ahmadabad, although it was quite hairy.

There was never – until we reached a village just after halfway – a straight part of the road for more than 20 yards. I noticed the driver's wheel had a black rubber cover on. It was covered in multi-coloured knobs, for easy-grip. You could see his Mum giving it to him for his birthday. It reminded me of the fancy Durex, the sort that reaches the parts others don't, that one hears about – protection for steering wheels – in this case a prophelactic against premature death.

About halfway up we stopped. Still no-one spoke. There was a café-cum-shop perched on the side of a steep drop – let's face it, everything's perched on the side of a steep drop. There were loos – I declined the opportunity – and on the other side of the road a house with a lovely little girl standing in the doorway. As I stretched my legs I smiled at her. She half-hid round the door. I knew in my bag I'd a few pens and little girls love anything to write with. It was my only spare one. A nice purple colour. I went over and gave it to her. She disappeared pretty quickly and I wondered at the conversation she had with her mother inside their far-flung home in the Himalayas, about a strange woman giving out pens for nothing. As I boarded the jeep again – one more shove – they both appeared at the door smiling and waving. It was a great day to be up the Himalayas even if I didn't know as yet how many of us would make it. Since the events as we left town, no-one else had had the misfortune to slip. They must have a grip like a vice to stay on.

Once we passed the halfway stage, wild monkeys, whole families of them started appearing at the side of the road. As we'd come up to one family, a baby had got hold of a blue plastic bag and was chewing it, so the chances of it growing into a photogenic tourist attraction were looking a bit dim. Due to the risks to wildlife the authorities in Darjeeling were trying to get shopkeepers to revert to paper bags but only a few of the better shops seemed to do it.

All the way up there were houses perched precariously on all the hillsides, which seemed to be terraced paddy fields. Some were on stilts, with the front stilts being longer as they went down into the edge of the hillside. Their views were spectacular. The air was clear, not too crisp though. The only pollution would be the varying jeeps and vehicles necessary for day-to-day functions. Now and again you would see a child walking, going uphill, with a school bag, to where, who knows? From where? Exactly.

Eventually we reached a small town or large village, Kurseong. By now the people no longer seemed Indian. They had taken on a Nepalese/Tibetan look. Very few women wore saris, whether because a bare midriff was not conducive to life in the mountains, I don't know. Men were appearing in suits, often with v-necked sweaters beneath. They had a distinct look of 'Man at C & A' circa 1970. Charles Bronson wouldn't have looked out of place here. His slimmed-down looks were everywhere. Others looked like many photos of gurkha soldiers you see, but no-one looked Indian.

Through the town we came to a halt. I then realized it was 3.30pm and a private school was disgorging its pupils. I try and miss school finish times at home whenever I can, and there I was caught up in the Indian sub-continents version of car-hell. There were the small Ducati vans with boys in their hot, woollen blazers all over the place. There was one road through the town with traffic both ways. Well that was the plan but it seems that at 3.30 it goes into reverse for about 20 minutes. To be able to afford these mini–vans the families have to be rich and after that, they have to afford the schools. I wondered how many of the children were going home for the Christmas (Diwali) holidays or was this exodus an everyday event?

After the town and as we were nearing Darjeeling, small villages began springing up. People started to leave the jeep, one here, one there. Talk started for the first time. Desultorily at first and then more animated.

I'd noticed as we hit these villages, the railway line was running right by the side of the road and the shops seemed to have their wares displayed almost to the edge of the line. So it wasn't electric then. It was one of the last narrow gauge railways.

People seemed to be shopping in the same Christmas Eve frenzy as in the UK. Garlands of marigold and fairy lights were everywhere. Having noticed the railway line, I saw people walking along it, chatting. An 18 month old child staggered along beside it – totally unaccompanied – would it make 2, given the proximity of the road and the railway? Well apparently it would. A hoot of the whistle and this enormous train lumbered into view. It was full size – on the lines of our railways in the 60s – and proceeded to pass by the shops and their goods and more importantly the children in their nappies. The children of India appear to be as well trained (excuse the pun) and as laid back as the animals. Is there something they know we can give our children who are a little more hyperactive than the drug Ritalin? Is it the smell from the Poinsettia trees/shrubs that are all over the place? Can't be that, I've only seen them up here and the children in India generally are placid.

Is it the fact that they are allowed to stay up until they fall asleep where they are and are then carried to their beds? The older ones are walked to bed. Children are not considered a nuisance in India. Everything is put into their well-being. They are the family's investment in the future.

Back to the jeep, once the talk started, the guy opposite me filled me in with what had been going on – re the unfortunate faller by the wayside and so much else. It turned out my informant was a guide and he'd just taken his last lot of tourists back to the airport and he was on holiday for Diwali. His name was Namgyal and he worked for Sherpa Tensing's – he made the first ascent of Everest with Edmund Hillary – sons with their Adventure Trekking Co. I liked the sound of adventure trekking. It didn't sound like a coach tour. Tell me more.

He could arrange for me to travel further up the Himalayas in two days time after my stay in Darjeeling. I would need a permit as this was a restricted area due to its proximity through the Himalayas to Tibet (China), Nepal, Bhutan and Bangladesh. I could have my own jeep and my own guide. I really did like it, do tell more.

Well the next day, as he was off, would I like him to

show me Darjeeling and take me to the Tibetan Refugee centre? Is the Pope a Catholic? I made a date with my new friend and told him to come up with some figures for the expedition as I like to think of it.

So you see I could survive. You know the saying, if I fell in a pile of shit, I'd come up smelling of roses — well, at a price.

We were dropping people off in the villages as we approached Darjeeling, and I realized we were in the 'suburbs'. Eventually village merged into village and then we were downtown. This was a serious disappointment. It was scruffy, dingy and nowhere near a romantic-looking destination. I thought this was where the memsahibs from Calcutta and Lucknow hung out through the long hot summers, this being the oldest hill station in India.

I was dropped among a load of jeeps, all looking better than the one I've arrived in. I hailed a taxi (on Namgyal's directions,) and proceeded to my 4 star hotel.

As we were in the Himalayas all roads led up and down quite severely. My taxi headed on up. I'd got both my bags but have to say the one on the roof-rack was hanging precariously by one strap over the side as I collected it. I think Amex got lucky there.

As we climbed higher up the 9 in 10 hill, the American western town/bazaar effect disappeared and decent shops started to show. Finally we hit a bit of a plateau and it seemed like a square with tea-rooms, souvenir shops and views of ordinary mountains. There were a few donkeys and guides. So this was where all the tourist action was at.

CHAPTER NINETEEN

Bedroom fires and hot bottles

My hotel was a former gentlemen's residence. There were roaring fires, smoke rooms, bar, numerous lounges, conservatory; and I don't mean the sort we tag onto our houses – plus a verandah. My room was beautiful, like a Victorian drawing room. And the views were spectacular over Darjeeling and mountains. Spectacular, that's a word which may become over-used in the Himalayas.

The cost of this hotel including all meals and afternoon tea was £30.00 per day. I'd never be at home if I could get this rate in England. Also the room had a TV and a mini-bar. At night the staff came to make up and light your fire – light my fire – you're talking to someone who needs air conditioning in the loo. It still didn't stop them putting a hot water bottle in my bed when I was off-guard having dinner. They'd seemed surprised when I refused the fire – I need to spray with Evian water three times a night when I sleep under just a sheet.

Well, what a surprise, guess who came to dinner? – the Cox and Kings' brigade! I bet they weren't paying £15.00 per night for a shared room. Their tour guide was a particularly unpleasant Indian man who felt he should give them all the benefit of his philosophy – a woman's place is in the home etc. As he said, a view not so popular in England. He then patronized them all by teasing them about where they were going the next day. They, these good, educated, classy people from middle-England, reacted like schoolchildren. I don't think they were hanging on his every word – he'd alienated at least half of them with his kitchen remark, but of course they were lumbered with him and had to make the best of a bad job. I think the more independent minded amongst them resented him completely. Some of the looks he was getting. I was so GLAD I was on my own.

They were off to a tea plantation and if they were good, he'd give them more details in due course. Pass the sick bag Mavis. I was beginning to feel rather superior. I had paid very little to be there and I could do what I wanted and go where I wanted. The joy of it.

The hotel seemed to be half Hindu and half Buddhist. Everyone, and I mean everyone, celebrated Diwali. There seemed to be a fusion of religions in the mountains. People didn't seem to belong to one definitive faith. There were clear fairy lights all the way round the roof of the hotel which was sprawled over quite an acreage just clinging to the rock face. Didn't know if that was for Diwali or was normal. Bowls of marigolds were everywhere, statues were adorned with them and they floated in any water there might be. Garlands of them decorated the main statues of Gods.

Namgyal (his name means king) came to collect me after breakfast. His first job was to take me shopping. I presumed this was either (a) to get his commission later or (b) to support some relative in the manner to which they'd become accustomed. Anyway I enjoyed it. The first was a jewellery and souvenir shop. There were some lovely dress rings with semi-precious stones set in silver. I ordered a few. On my return later I would buy a silk Buddhist wall hanging.

Next we got a warm Himalayan jacket. I would need

it for the next stage of my journey. Shopping done, we headed off to the Tibetan Refugee Centre. Nam's mother was a Tibetan refugee, so naturally he had an affinity for the place. It was perched on the other side of the top town. Some of the buildings had corrugated roofs. Tibetan flags flew all over the place. First I saw the kitchens, an enormous aluminium pan, or say casserole dish about 30" across, was in the centre. Namgyal said they catered for 600 people who lived there, but this could be 2,000 per day with people who came and went, all supported the centre in some way, working with them.

The buildings seemed to be arranged round an inner yard, about 35' wide 70' long. When I was there boys varying from about 5 to 12 years old were playing cricket with makeshift stumps and even a makeshift bat. The ball was rather big and could have doubled as a football in an emergency – but they were very enthusiastic and when you smiled at them, they went all coy and shy. Beautiful sunny children. There was a big sign over one of the main buildings that said, Tibetan Refugee Orphanage. I should imagine if you have to be orphaned anywhere, this would be the best place for any child.

We entered another shed. There was coarse wool all over and old ladies – they looked 90 but could have been nearer my age for all I knew – were knitting or wearing it. They smiled. Toothless, friendly smiles. I would imagine they still speak their own tongue. Living amongst your own people there's no incentive to learn a new language at the wrong time of life. The whole enterprise seemed to be not unlike a co-operative.

We then went into the shop. Quite light and airy. A long L-shaped counter. There were "Free Tibet" t-shirts on the wall, also wood carvings of dragons and intricate designs. Some knitted gloves and socks. I bought up their stock. I didn't realize I was doing it but anyone who's been shopping with me knows that to clear the stock of my chosen shop has often been my desire. It was only when they said they didn't have any more of this or that it dawned on me that the poor old ladies (there were some younger ones) were going to have to go into overdrive to refurbish the shop. The two t-shirts were the only shirts. The gloves, the socks, the same. Even the carvings. I looked round despairingly to see how to increase my contribution. So I left a donation and departed. Namgyal carried my purchases. A true gentleman. At 1.00pm we parted company and he went back to his family for the celebrations.

In the afternoon I decided to visit an observation tower and did feel that a Sherpa should have been in attendance or at least some oxygen should have been offered along the route. As I arrived that night, and the next morning I had a bit of altitude sickness – felt light-headed – but it soon cleared. At the observation post we were meant to be able to see the third highest mountain in the world, but it was cloudy. There were monkeys all over the place – certainly more clued-up than the tourists. Buddhist prayer flags fluttered. There were many tourists. As I made my way down an old man, bearded mystic-type, beckoned me. Well allowing I could run faster than him, I followed him down 62 steps – greater love has no man – round corners until I came to his ashram. Candles, monkeys, marigolds – I took my shoes off and approached. He said, "Baksheesh" as I expected and I gave him 10 rupees. He seemed pleased, anointed me with orange

dye on my hair, gave me a marigold and off I went. As
I started back up the 62 steps (at altitude) he caught
hold of me and tried to get me to go further down the
steps. I wasn't having any of this, so I smiled nicely,
pulled myself away and climbed smartly up.

As I reached, with relief, the path at the top, the
big monkey, head honcho I'd photographed on the
way up, sprang at me, bared its teeth and growled. I
threw him the marigold. I thought he'd be as interested as the baby monkeys who were eating them
were, but I think they eat anything just like human
babies. Marigold card already played – just my camera left. I swung it round my head and it backed off
but by then I was snarling too. You don't have five
children without developing a heightened sense of
survival instinct. As I went down it was just starting
to attack a family.

Later I took myself off for my picture to be taken. I
needed this for the permit for Sikkim province.
Namgyal had returned with his brother and given me
the figures for my escorted trip. It would be £160.00.
This was for four days accommodation, all food
included, my guide for five days, and my own jeep or
similar. I could visit anywhere I wanted. Just tell the
driver. Now I know I could have got this figure down,
but by UK standards it was excellent value. Namgyal
said the hotel in Gangtok would have spectacular views.
He promised. I made a feeble attempt at negotiations
but my heart wasn't in it, so we agreed on £150.00.

I left the top mall where all the good hotels were
and started down the descending high street. A rather
large store was selling candles, films, breathtaking
views of the Himalayas and t-shirts and also had a
photographer tucked away in the back. This nice

young man took me into a room at the back, all decked out with huge umbrellas as though for a Kate Moss photo-shoot. For £1.00 I got 8 photos, which looked to have taken 20 years off me. He posed me and although he didn't say all the Bailey things to make me sparkle, something worked. The only downside was that immediately after, whilst I was browsing in the shop, my 8 pictures were posted up on a large advertising board, at ceiling height, similar to the display at the entrance to The Big One at Blackpool. A bit disconcerting and rather an ordeal whilst I was still around. There's not much can stop me from shopping but I think they've discovered it at altitude in the Himalayas. I was out of there pretty quick.

I was taking a 36 roll of film a day at the time. Thought I'd need a bank loan to get them all developed and I'd not hit Rajasthan yet, which was where I was always heading.

I collected all my morning shopping plus a few extras, cashed a traveller's cheque – no mean feat – and headed back to my hotel up the hill in the dark. I was half-expecting to be mugged but nothing happened and I arrived back at my hotel safe and sound. Namgyal said his people are a peaceful people. I believed him.

Early evening Namgyal and his brother appeared again with my itinerary, money changed hands and the deal was done. Namgyal looked very like my eldest son, but so had half the town. All the babies looked like him when my son was their age. Allowing I know who my son's father was, it was all very strange.

I went in for my dinner, the whole hotel was lit only by candlelight for Diwali – the festival of light. This was so romantic but just how romantic I was to realize later. There were to be fireworks at the hotel, but naturally they were all over town as well. This was their big day.

The menu was unexciting. The Cox and Kings' tour was being duly patronized by the chauvinistic, smug tour leader. Everything was normal. I had the chicken, the same as I had at lunch as it was quite mild. It was only when I got to the last piece and was cutting it up that in the dim glooming I saw the blood running out of it. I double checked. Too late now. I retired to my room.

By 10.00pm I knew just how romantic those candles were and why someone told me later they always ate vegetarian in India. They'd seen the abattoirs and they wouldn't eat meat until they hit England again.

It had taken four weeks, but Delhi Belly had finally claimed me for its own.

And so started a quite spectacular acquaintance with Thomas Crapper's most famous invention, that lasted from 10.00pm until dawn.

CHAPTER TWENTY

Kachenjunga is clear

I awoke feeling washed out. My legs were unsteady and my stomach was still convulsing. The pain if I were a masochist was exquisite.

I gave breakfast a miss and at 10.00 am my driver and van arrived. That's right, van. The jeep I had been expecting had transformed itself overnight into a Maruti van (a narrow mini–van). The driver looked like every gurkha you'd ever seen in those old black and white war films. Since I knew they were on our side, this generated confidence in me, soon dispelled when I realized he didn't speak English.

Allowing for the fact that I was doubled-up in pain (this was explained by the hotel owner to him) and had no way of making my intentions known, it looked like being a long 5 days.

He was a good driver and this seemed essential as were going another 4½ hours, further up the Himalayas and it was even worse than the first part to Darjeeling. Now in many places the road had almost disappeared due to landslides and general erosion during the rainy season.

I groaned quietly sitting on the rear seat with my feet up and a cushion at my back. Despite everything I still had my camera at the ready. The intrepid tourist, although due to all the things that have and are happening I feel that intrepid explorer would be more appropriate.

I know I wasn't crossing burning deserts on a camel with a tribe of Bedouins to an unknown destination, but allowing I ached all over, was bored, felt all round dreadful and the ruts in the endless road jarred my very being, I must qualify as being more than just a tourist.

There were not as many hairpin bends this time, but you were still hurled around. The scenery was different and if it weren't for the high peaks of the Himalayas peeking through the clouds now and again you could feel you were in the less-stark parts of the Trough of Bowland. They'd even got English weeds, but then there was Hibiscus or Poinsettia to make it feel more exotic. Not long after we set off we had to stop at a type of border post. The Indian Army controlled this and it was there that my driver would get me my permit. The maximum was for 15 days although this varies from time to time and is usually used by those going trekking on the lower slopes of the Himalayas. Mine was only for 4 days so I shouldn't invite too much scrutiny. One look at me and they'd know I wouldn't pose much of a threat for organizing an invasion through the mountains.

Sikkim province, I was just about to enter, was a kingdom until Indira Gandhi decided it was a politically sensitive area and was too important to leave to the defence of a little kingdom in 1975. There was a bloodless coup. Sikkim covers only 2,800 square miles and is now India's twenieth state. Lepcha is the name for the indigenous population but now they are outnumbered by Tibetans and Nepalis and it was discontent from the immigrants that prompted Indira Gandhi to protect both them and one of India's most sensitive borders.

It's sensitive because it is bordered by Tibet (now officially called China on the main world maps),

Nepal, Bhutan and Bangladesh. The Indians fear an invasion, (mainly by China) and the place bristled with Army personnel.

People no longer looked like my eldest son, but now had a darker skin with Indian/Bhutanese looks. The photos I took on the way up showed bridges which looked like an HGV would finish them off, when I knew they regularly hosted these vehicles, Army as well as delivery trucks. On one particular bridge was a large yellow sign proclaiming that the army maintained the bridge in the service of the nation. I presumed the border was better protected than the bridge was maintained. Above that was a metal tourist information triangle with two peaks of the Himalayas and blue sky above. A goat meandered along just beneath it. At one point we came to a full stop as sitting in the middle of the road was a very young kid. It didn't look injured but it wasn't going anywhere either. It had that calm, placid look of an Indian animal. Either nothing could harm it or its karma would decide. Troops of monkeys still patrolled the sides of the road, nervous young ones peeped over the parapets as we passed. I took many pictures of where most of the road just disappeared down a ravine. This distracted me from the pain and discomfort. After all adrenaline kills pain. I have to admit for most of the journey, it just seemed like an endless twisting for my aching body. How can anyone spend four weeks in India without succumbing to Delhi belly and get it at a 4 star hotel? Well now I knew – wonder how Cox and Kings' lot were faring? Would their guide be telling them they'd all been very naughty and they had to miss all the treats he had in store to stay in bed with a hot water bottle and a roaring fire until they were better?

At the border post I got out of my van and headed for the café whilst my guide organized a permit. I sat in front of a bowl of soup – untouched – and sipped a Coca-Cola. I just wanted to be in a comfy bed. When my guide returned to me I was nearly asleep, face down in my soup. I jolted myself awake and climbed, very light-headed, into the van.

I'd learned to say Dillytasha to the Tibetans and join my hands and bow. They smiled a lot, whether in sympathy at my accent or they were just pleasant people, I don't know.

At one point my guide stopped the van and motioned for me to get out. Must I? This was a vantage point. A tourist stop. Other people (Indians) were there. I duly got my camera and went and stood inside the summer house structure with seats. I just wanted to sit down. No, I had to look. And there far below me I saw a river. Not one though, two rivers, one joining the other. The one joining was green, the flowing one was blue. This was the meeting of the Ranjit (green) and Teesta (blue) rivers. Ranjit is the male joining the female. For all I know this could be fluvial coitus or fluvial coitus interruptus. I realized I was witnessing something symbolic, but how symbolic to me would only become clear later.

After, 4½ long hours we twisted our way into Gangtok, another cowboy western looking town. Many of the buildings had huge supports jutting out of the rocks to balance the building on the edge of a dramatic drop some hundreds of feet below. As we'd come up many houses were suspended in this way and as we approached Gangtok one or two had succumbed and were beginning a hesitant precarious crumbling to whoever or whatever lay those many hundred feet

Dipti and myself, ready for anything but the stick dance

Myself, Barry, Dani, Priscilla and Benita

Building site, Indian style. Safety measures, also Indian style

Health and safety inspector on the right (4 legs a prerequisite)

Leaving Bandra Railway station, Bombay

Taj Mahal Hotel, Bombay. Opposite the Gateway to India

Elephanta Isle stalls and salesmen extraordinaire

Barry, myself and Dipti. Bombay trip

Dipti and Sanjay, Goa

The temple erected at the apartment for the visit of a holy man

Arrivals lobby, Coconut Lagoon

Departure lobby, Coconut Lagoon

Waterways Life, Kerala

View from the houseboat, irrigation canals on the waterways

Endangered Keralan elephant

My bungalow at Marari Beach

Hotel in Darjeeling

Tibetan refugee centre

Refugee centre

Refugee centre

Kitchen, refugee centre

Library at Buddhist monastery

Smiles of relief, dry land

View from upper Darjeeling

'Your home away from home'

Desert village

Workers at the marble factory

Jain temple and walking tourist cliché

The inner sanctum, Jain temple

Inside the fortress, Jaisalmer

Oasis of calm, road to Jodhpur

The Maharajah with the wandering eyes

Crowded Palace, Udaipur

The boys, being proper tourists in Jaipur

Hali Aji Temple, Bombay

Next door neighbour, Hemman, wife, Dipti, Barry (moustache shaved off for 40th birthday) next door neighbour and various children

below. There didn't seem to be any contingency plans for dismantling them to make them safe. But I was only a tourist, what did I know?

As is usual in this part of the world, we parked on a hill, which in this case was the drive into the hotel Netuk House. Nam had promised me fantastic views. I have to admit this was the last thing on my mind, but as I made my way to my room I remembered thinking, "Some view," and felt I'd been sold a pup along with my non-English speaking guide.

Easing my pain-filled body out of the van I was greeted in beautiful English by a lovely man. "Welcome to my hotel Mrs Buckley. Oh dear, are you all right?" I gasped how nice to be greeted in English – he said he was educated by the Christian Brothers (they get everywhere) – and that I wasn't feeling too good and just wanted my bed. I also still had enough wits about me to say I wouldn't need my non-English speaking guide the next day. I was feeling slightly better already. There's nothing like taking control of your life on one hand whilst surrendering completely on the other. I felt I could trust my new host. There was no better place to be ill. He was most anxious about me and solicitous to say the least. Lead me to my room.

We went up and onto a wide 14ft x 30ft long terrace. The rooms were arranged like a motel really. All connected, six giving onto the terrace with another six above them. The room was smallish, cool with a single bed against a wall, at the back was a shower room and loo. The walls were pale yellow, with stencils in red and green of what seemed to be tulips. The floor was tiled with a woven rug by the bed. It looked like a luxury sanctuary in an exclusive retreat.

My host asked would I like anything? I asked for just a banana but a bowl of fruit and mineral water arrived. For some reason I felt spoiled. He said he would send soup about 7.00pm and to have a nice rest. I gratefully sank into bed. It was just 3.30pm. I slept beautifully until a knock at the door heralded a young man who took his job seriously. He duly presented me with soup, dry toast and mineral water. It was perfect. The green vegetable soup I couldn't identify was as good as I've ever tasted. Smooth, not too rich.

I read for a bit and then tried to sleep again. Not as easy this time because Gangtok must be where they did quarrying in this part of the world. It felt like they were blasting well into the night. My room shuddered. It was midnight before it dawned on me that it was fireworks for Diwali. As I became more conscious I realized the noise was coming from every direction and then I knew I wasn't in the middle of a quarry. It's strange what tricks the mind plays when you're exhausted and semi-conscious. Through the hotel I heard English voices. Quite distant, on the rooftop. There was also an unusual noise of drunken revellers, sounding like any UK town centre on a Saturday night. Didn't know Indian youths got so rowdy, so out of character from what I know of India. I was curious to know what was going on, but too tired to find out.

The next morning at 7.00am there was a knock at my door. I peeked round the gap I'd opened to see the serious young man with a beaker, a top in place and a well-rehearsed speech, "Kachenjunga is clear." I thanked him and repeated it to myself.

The brain was beginning to clear, sleep had worked its usual miracle. Kachenjunga after Everest and K2 was the third highest mountain in the world. It was clear. That must mean something.

I opened my door, and before me – I felt I could touch it – was Kachenjunga. It was big. Big, pointed and mine. There was only me on the terrace. I wanted to run along all the other doors and get them out. Surely they wanted to see it? I felt it was one of the most awe-inspiring moments of my life. I felt privileged. It was majestic, beautiful, spectacular. I rushed to get my camera. I did my best to preserve it for perpetuity. Still no-one joined me. Kanchenjunga is clear. With that pronouncement I did not realize that I was hearing a most unusual statement, but as I watched a cloud moved in gracefully – spitefully? – and covered it once more. And that was how it stayed for the rest of my trip as it had been before I arrived. It dazzles for so little time, a butterfly of the Himalayas. The third largest butterfly in the world.

My tea sat untouched. I wasn't hungry but life felt good again. The aches had more or less gone and hopefully I'd lost weight.

I appeared at breakfast to be greeted by my host Pem Namgyal. He seemed pleased I'd recovered but I just asked for my usual plain omelette, I always revert to this in times of stomach upset. The most delightful, light omelette quickly appeared. I had some toast, Coca-Cola – so good for sickness, used in hospitals – and left.

I asked Pem to arrange sightseeing in a jeep with an English speaking guide to take me to a Buddhist Monastery. A nice young man turned up and we set off. I've since found that all monasteries require you to park about ¾ mile from the building and walk, always up a hill. Their own vehicles of course are allowed up. My driver parked and pointed the way, I grimaced. I might be feeling better but it was now midday again, and Noel Coward where art though? And the sun and weakness made me feel like I was climbing Everest without oxygen.

I reached the top to find an enormous amount of building surrounding gardens, courtyards. I was not able to have a conducted tour as the trainee priests were at instruction. I was taken in through to the back of a class where I could see the youngsters sitting crossed-legged on the floor listening intently. Not all the trainees were young, some were evidently in their 20s, these I presumed to be near the end of their training. For those who weren't in lessons, it was lunchtime. Now you don't think that someone who is studying in such a rarefied atmosphere conforms to the norm of set mealtimes.

I turned the usual prayer wheels and then visited the library. So different from ours. There were ladders on runners to reach the top, beautiful, polished wooden shelves and drawers, but the "books" were different. They were boxes of different colours – a bit like when our children are starting to read and they work their way up to the hardest colour – with the appropriate coloured ribbons hanging off them and a label with details. The colours spectred like a rainbow, with orange, fading to yellow and then into green and so on. It was a pleasing, calming effect.

The monastery itself was ornate on the outside with intricate plaques and inlaid patterns in rich colours. Prayer flags flew all over. Other buildings housed the students. It all appeared to be self-sufficient. There were children, boys naturally, about 5 or 6. They seemed to be having fun. Just as giggly and mischievous as western lads. There was more than one large obelisk-type edifice. The main one was surrounded by large red flags on poles, beneath these were the prayer wheels. Beside this sat a very colourful HGV but this one had been devoted to Buddha. Two young students sat in front playing a game in the pathway.

Throughout the gardens there were many centre-pieces, some in water, all ornamented. As I strolled, I met a family from Gujarat – this was their holiday period for their Christmas – and we chatted. They asked could we all have our picture taken together. It wasn't worth explaining that I ruined more pictures that I have ever made, so they took me and them together. I reciprocated and got someone to take one with my camera. Actually in my version I wouldn't stop traffic, hopefully theirs is the same.

Having done my cultural bit, I started off back down the road. On my right a little boy, about 7, was just going into his house, thatched roof, once again perched precariously on the side of the mountain. He was followed by a chicken, then a couple of hens. It also looked as though the goats had the run of the place too. Still, it was in an idyllic place.

I asked my guide to take me back then. I was feeling very tired. So we set off to a CD of Smokie singing Needles and Pins and other latest releases!

I've noticed there are quite a few independent travellers about my age. None I've met so far are British. I'm very pleased though with Nam for the hotel, despite the van and non-English speaking guide.

CHAPTER TWENTY ONE

Would you like to body surf the rapids?

On my return Smokie still ringing in my ears, I met Pem. He greeted me as graciously as usual, I commented on the beautiful food I had received albeit only soup and omelette. He said that his wife was in charge of the kitchen and she was very fussy.

We chatted a while and he offered me a book which recalled the last days of the kingdom. His father had been a court official to the king – I think he was a foreign minister. I read the Sikkim Kingdom, which took up just a chapter, during my afternoon siesta.

There were two other women at the hotel, one Swiss and one German, travelling together. He said we all might like to view a film of the local gurkha soldier, holder of the VC.

So that evening after dinner we three presented ourselves in his living room and sat, surrounded by Pem's children, and watched a 20 minute video on a very brave man who, not only distinguished himself in war, but changed his village's life for the better. The film was in English. After the soldier returned to his country he set about establishing a school in his village and using his notoriety to generally improve everyone's lot locally. He died in the eighties, a man content with his achievements.

Talking with Pem in the afternoon, I'd mentioned my desire to go white water rafting – so I must've been feeling better. He said it would be possible when we went back down if enough people wanted to go. It would be expensive to hire a raft on my own. I was more concerned with how I'd paddle it. I'd have to work bloody hard. There was a grave possibility of my going round in circles.

He was telling me that he'd had a German guy who wanted a room. When he'd shown him to the simple oasis I'd fallen in love with and told him it was £30.00 inc per day, the guy went mad and said it wasn't worth it. Pem just stated "Sometimes simplicity costs money."

I think I met the guy later, well I certainly heard him. He was in the room above me with a young Indian woman. He was either very energetic or he'd drawn the noisiest bed in the oasis, oh, yes, and he shouted at her a lot – I think, or p'raps he was just a very loud lover. Every time they returned to their room, the headboard seemed to bang against the wall rhythmically. My only comment is I think he was quicker than the report on JFK's speed in the bedroom. So that's not the biggest compliment I could give him.

At breakfast the next day I think he spoke to me. Heavy German accent, 6ft 4in tall, thick set, about 50. She said nothing and eventually melted away presumably back to their room. He then gave me the inside track on him. The hotel, his relationship, Indians and for all I can remember – Adolf Hitler. It appeared he was Austrian, working in Delhi. His opinion of Indians was somewhere above pavement level. Said they trusted no-one because they couldn't trust each other. Were suspicious of everyone and resented him because he had an Indian girlfriend and she was much younger than he. They didn't like that. The hotel price was too high, he objected to paying it. His tirade finished, I said nothing. About his racist opinions, his staying power or noisy bedhead. I just presumed we'd nothing in common.

I had found Pem to be a lovely, calm, erudite, informative, caring man. A nice interlude and worth the trip further up the Himalayas, to visit both him and his hotel. I still think of it longingly.

After two days I was awaiting my van to collect me after breakfast. Pem had sent into the village for some more "tummy pills" as mine had run out. They arrived just as I was leaving. Then Pem placed a long, silk scarf around my neck and bowed in the traditional way and said his goodbyes. Clutching my lifesavers, still feeling ropy, we were off, lurching down the upright hills of Gangtok. Yep, the houses which were starting their descent the quick way down to the bottom seemed to be at the same stage as 48 hours earlier. So it's a slow-moving affair.

That day, in India, it was Brother's Day. This is taken seriously by all Indians even those who have relocated to other countries. I don't believe there is a Sister's Day but that didn't surprise me.

Brother's Day means sisters do all the work for their brothers. They buy them presents and all day the brothers get treated like kings. I saw many men – most below the age of 30 – garlanded with marigolds and jogging along in the back of carts going somewhere exciting. Some were just walking alone, by the roadside – but their garlands were evident. Excitement was in the air. Those in the carts waved and laughed as they passed by – or in our case, as we passed them. It was quite infectious. Had I been born the wrong sex? Naah – I wouldn't swop, not even for Brother's Day.

All over India are the wish trees festooned with

ornaments, paper wishes and any manner of bits and bobs. These are wishes of the people for the Gods to grant their requests usually located near a temple. Sanjay informed me all about them when I asked him. The trimmings reach to the top no matter how high the tree. There were quite a few in the Himalayas and even in the middle of the streets in the big towns.

On leaving Gangtok we came down as fast as the bends would allow, passing the troops of monkeys, the odd child walking alone to what seemed to be nowhere. No houses, no buildings, just steep roads, bridges half-washed away and other roads half of which disappeared into the ravines with alarming regularity, especially on corners.

As we neared the bottom I could see the river now and again. I was on my way for one night only to Kalimpong. This was another hill station but slightly further down than Darjeeling. It would give me more options to sightsee and get the feel for other areas of the Himalayas.

As I saw the river getting closer I kept saying, very distinctly "Rafting. Rafting." On the way up through my pain haze I'd seen the adverts and knew we were near. If we started to climb, as we would, the chance would be lost. My guide (I once knew his name) seemed to be ignoring me. I tapped him on the shoulder, pointed at the river and said "Rafting," he didn't seem to understand.

At this stage in my life I had never been whitewater rafting and it looked like I wouldn't be starting then. Was this God's way of telling me I shouldn't? Was my illness his way of saying, "Don't do it, the time's not right, perhaps it never will be for you Pat Buckley, poor swimmer, scared of water, – back out now."

I know when I swim, always where my feet can

touch the bottom, I usually gasp, "Excuse me" to anyone in my way, as anytime I touch someone, I just go
under. It's very undignified. The family think it's hilarious.

I'd resigned myself to God's will when we stopped
suddenly outside a café. I gingerly clambered down,
tummy still not too good. Would I like something to
eat? Well not really, first Coca-Cola. The two young
lads running the place spoke English and my guide
just said to me – "Rafting." Other than 'Dillytasha' this
was the most we'd exchanged. Things were looking
up. I explained to the lads what I wanted to do and I
could see a brochure in English for rafting.

The efficiency is such in this part of the world that
within 20 minutes of my request to the lads for rafting, I was actually in a raft. I had been picked up in a
jeep by 2 laughing young guys, 2 young girls (around
12/15) and a family of 3 Indians. We raced to the river,
unloaded, were given life jackets, instructions on how
to paddle, had put all our worldly belongings in a
waterproof container and horrifyingly seen the rescue
methods.

I think "Rescue methods" could be prosecutable
under the Trades Descriptions Act if they had one. I'd
asked re: a helmet, but was told there were no rocks.
This was going to be a very strange river, almost
Disneyworld-like. Well I'd not died on the road to Hell,
it was not my time. Blow what the guide books said.
I'd not signed a disclaimer re: insurance in fact I'd not
heard that word mentioned – and I was far too excited
to ask.

The rescue method consisted of pink nylon cord
about ½" thick attached to a pink plastic drum which
it then fed out to the unfortunate rafter. The drum was

about 8in by 6in x 6in. This was thrown to you if you ended up overboard. The idea being that they reel you in. Oh, please, that I don't have to use it.

Having said that I was trying to imagine what it would be like. The ultimate thrill. That could be literal as ultimate indicates last.

Before we set off, the leader asked me if I would like to body surf the rapids. I looked round to see if he were talking to anyone else. No, I was the one he'd selected as being daft enough to undertake that particular feat.

I croaked an incredulous, "No" and his reply was that two English women a few weeks ago had done just that. I replied I bet they weren't my age. A bit of a weak excuse but he'd flummoxed me.

I think this is my year for – body surfing in Wales – discovering the Himalayas – "rickstaing" in Bombay – and now whitewater rafting. At least I'm not near Kashmiri rebels so I shouldn't be kidnapped. I'd told my family I was rafting, but it didn't matter, as by the time they received the letter it'd all be over – one way or the other.

We were seated by the "Leader" and I ended up on the left-side front, with the father of the family on the other side. His wife and son sat behind us. One of the guys went at the back as rudder to guide the raft towards the best rapids. The leader was sitting precariously on the side. His sisters seemed to be wherever they wanted – these were evidently people at ease on the river. Just us novices then with faster beating hearts.

We launched on our two hour trip. The scenery between rapids was stunning. We were on the Teesta river, the blue one, the female. I stuck one foot in the corner and had been told to head right over to the water when sculling. I was seated on the side, on top of it really. No wonder so many people end up in the water – you're halfway there, the rapids nearly have their job done for them. Given gravity, it takes very little to dislodge a slippy bum. I think your foot is in the corner as an anchor.

As we hit the first rapids, we stopped paddling as we'd been told and paddled backwards. I couldn't help singing the Hawaii 5 o theme tune. It was so noisy I don't think anyone heard me, but it made me feel good. Was I reclaiming my youth? I don't think so, I never did this in my youth. I remember a few tame holidays sunbathing and dancing but I don't remember a pink nylon rescue method coming into it, and oh yes, I may have paddled.

As we hit each rapid I realized that the only part of me still in the raft was my leg. So then the leader invited me once again to body surf the next rapids. Other English women do it he said. Well this one doesn't. So it fell to the Indian boy, about 17, to go over into the river. Please note, he did not body surf the rapids, he just bobbed about in blue water until the rescue method was thrown to him. I think the leader held the other end. It definitely was not attached to anything secure. I just marvelled at the casualness of it all. They pulled him towards the raft and you should have seen the palaver they had to get him back on board. They struggled, they wrestled, they hauled, pulled, grabbed – where's the Thesaurus? There must be many other words for how they tried to get him aboard. This was a fit 17 year old and two young guys and they still couldn't get him back. What hope for a middle-aged clog dancer? I'd still be there. After quite a tussle he manoeuvred himself aboard and his parents looked relieved. To prove how easy it was, one of the sisters, in her sari, launched herself over the side and didn't even need the rescue method to clamber back. Show-off. Towards the end the rudder guy at the back took the plunge and once again was back in, in seconds. But I have to say, not one of these people body surfed the rapids. I think that particular delicacy was saved for melodramatic English women – he must have spotted me as one of them.

About halfway down the trip we passed the point where the green male Ranjit river meets the blue female Teesta river, the one I'd seen from above two days earlier. I have to report, the earth didn't move for me but perhaps they were at the stage of enjoying a cigarette as I passed by.

The water with which we were drenched wasn't too cold, quite pleasant really but there wasn't a part of me that wasn't wet. Still, that's what I'd come for.

Two, dizzy, thrilling hours later we pulled into a sand and stone beach on the right. We clambered out, quite relieved. All those who hadn't wanted to go in, hadn't done and those that did, had got their kicks.

Apparently my van was waiting for me at the top of the hill. Not too bad a hill, especially allowing we were in the Himalayas. So I said goodbye, having had my photo taken as proof, I flapped my dripping wet body onwards and upwards. I was passed halfway up by the jeep with everyone else on board – now why hadn't I thought of that? By this time my shorts were chaffing my thighs nicely.

Puffing, panting, and nicely chaffed, I reached my driver. I staggered aboard and then realized because I'd come down the river we now had to go back across all the bridges we'd already traversed. All the dodgy ones. We finally made it to my new hotel for 2.30pm.

As I got out, wet and dishevelled, in front of the hotel, many people, coiffed, soignee and respectable, were sitting on the front lawn taking tea. They looked at me in disbelief and amusement. Had I a VPL? More than likely.

The receptionist greeted me and I was escorted to a downstairs bedroom, which in former days had been a salon and he ordered a drink and sandwiches for me. By now I had an appetite, no pains anywhere, but my chaffed thighs, and a zest for life I couldn't remember ever having before. I was invincible. I'm sure there's a Helen Reddy song about me somewhere.

I'd arranged with my driver via reception to be picked up for more sightseeing later that afternoon. I'd just eaten and showered when an alarmed receptionist rang me. There was a strike in Siliguri the next day when I was due to take my lunchtime flight. The whole town would be shut down from 6.00pm that night for 24 hours. There were no more flights as this was Friday until the Monday. Rajasthan was calling, the Himalayas were a spent force in my itinerary till next time, what did I want to do enquired reception?

He contacted my driver and we decided to make a run for it and see if we could get there before curfew. My belongings were loaded up again and we began our descent. So soon the bridges were beginning to nod as I passed by. I was like an old friend.

Corners were taken recklessly as we sped on. This was normally a four hour trip. It was nearly 3.00pm when we set off. We had to get to the airport side of the town to be ok. Also my driver had to be out the other side before 6.00pm or he'd be marooned 24 hours not earning.

It was nearly dark as we hit the flat. There were pro-
cessions and street parades everywhere. Town on
strike, who cares, it's the holidays. People were racing
everywhere dressed in the finest clothes. Saris
encrusted and glittering, flowing, colourful. There
were carts carrying more than one family and an exciting buzz in the town. Nothing to do with the strike – a
funfair was just being passed by a large procession
bearing one of the major Gods, which I think was Lord
Vishnu. Car horns were hooting and all manner of
instruments being blown. It was the Notting Hill
Carnival, Siliguri style. It was wonderful but we could-
n't get through. We were still the wrong side for the
airport. Finally at 5.30pm we got to the hotel nearest to
the airport. I stood patiently waiting for the people
ahead of me to check in. It was going to be ok. Such
relief.

Well it was until the man informed me that that was
the last room that he'd just given out. People were
arriving from all over now demanding rooms. We
could hardly get out of the grounds, vehicles were
everywhere, blocking, tooting, abandoned.

We got the van out and stopped to ring various
hotels in town. All were full. I think one was called
Cinderella's. By now I'd have taken a room in one
called "Dracula's."

We asked a man near the phone box re: accommodation and he thought the town was full but there
would be room in the hotels on the Nepal Road. We
were only 20 miles away from Nepal itself. Suddenly
my driver, he of no English said, "Road to Nepal bad –
no go, dangerous." I didn't try because I'm sure he
wouldn't tell me but exactly what was dangerous? The
roads or bandits. I like to think it was bandits. I'd done
the dangerous road bit. What a time to find out he

understood. He then said, "Try Sinclairs."

So we tried Sinclairs. It was a huge hotel and strangely it had rooms even though it was on the right side for the airport. I found out why. It smelt. A manager I spoke to said they had had a flood and had just opened after months of closure. So at least that explained the stench from the carpets. The air-conditioning just seemed to circulate it.

I said goodbye to my driver, tipped him well and realized he'd only 10 minutes to get to the other side of town. I often wonder did he make it? Still I'm sure he'd have relatives somewhere to bed down with.

Despite the smell, the room was clean, but I just couldn't bring myself to bathe in the huge, dark green marble bath. I left in a taxi with relief the next morning and arrived at the airport for 9.00am. My flight was after 1.00pm. The airport provided vouchers for breakfast for everyone – rather nice since it wasn't their fault – and I caught up on a lot of reading.

There was no sign of the Cox and Kings' brigade.

CHAPTER TWENTY TWO

My knight in shining armour

There was a flight from Bagdogra to Delhi but I couldn't use it due to my spare bag being left at my Calcutta airport hotel, so I lost a day in effect.

I arrived at Calcutta with 4 hours to spare before check-in to Delhi, so I negotiated with a taxi driver to give me a conducted tour of as much of Calcutta as we could manage in the allotted time.

I shared the cab originally from the airport with an Indian family going downtown and he charged them 450 rupees. I'd already arranged that that was the price I'd pay for my tour. At first he said, "You say," for the price. This made me feel I was both buyer and seller, but in reality I was really just "mug." He first took me to a most beautiful temple. People were streaming in and out. I'd noticed this. No matter what time of the day, most temples had many worshippers. It was by far the biggest temple I had seen. It was very ornate, the inside glittered and all the major Gods were painted flamboyantly on the walls. Each one had a melodramatic look to them. Their eyes in particular heavily made-up.

Due to the heavy traffic we only could go to certain areas or we would become snarled up in queues. So this brought us to the Science Park. I left the driver talking to other drivers, paid my entrance fee and wandered.

I bought an ice lolly and a Coke, (this I had been drinking since my encounter with the Diwali chicken). There was a cinema-type building which I presumed was showing scientific projects, but I didn't have enough time for that. A lot of it was the type of thing that open days in High Schools offer in the science lab, but in this case, quite large.

As I knew I'd only so long I was clock watching and decided to locate my taxi and return to the hotel, collect my case, and arrive in good time at the airport.

It wasn't too difficult locating my driver, as I recognized my Harrods bag on the back seat. We arrived at the airport at 5.20pm. He then began his whinge dance. How could I only give him 450 rupees, when the family had been willing to pay that for the 45 minute trip downtown. He wanted 850 rupees. Where was all this smiling and "You say" business? Had he had a personality transplant. Was India ahead of us once again in modern research and medical science? I compromised and gave him 600 rupees, allowing that a lot of the time he was waiting and not using his precious fuel.

As I wheeled my trolley through the entrance doors, the board flickered and it informed a very amazed – nay, shell shocked—me, that my flight to Delhi was not only boarding but just as quickly, the gate had closed.

Panic overwhelmed me. It wasn't due to leave until 7.30pm. This was the last flight of the day and I raced towards the x-ray machines. No chance they said.

All my carefully laid plans for Agra and the Taj Mahal by 11.00 am the next day were in ruins. Who'd done this to me? Well it appeared I had. The plane was due to leave at 17.30pm not 7.30pm. I'd been foiled by the 24 hour clock – not for the first time, I may add, in my life. My husband used to laugh at me. I had terrible trouble with 14.00 and 4.00, 17.00 and 7.00, 20.00 and 10.00. And you see he was right to laugh, it proved to be catastrophic.

Well ok, not really. I presented myself looking like a demented hen pushing a trolley at the airport manager's office.

What a nice man. "Madam please do not worry, it will be all right." And strangely enough I believed him – and it was. He seemed quite thrilled to see me, one must presume he was anticipating a boring evening and here he could be knight in shining armour and rescue a damsel in distress.

I had not to worry because tomorrow I could leave directly for Agra, no need to go through Delhi, and still arrive for mid morning. Ah yes, but I'd already left Calcutta once and I was only allowed to pass through en route this time. No problem, he would sort that.

I thanked him profusely as I began to resemble a human being again and not a wet, dripping rag. He assured me that this was his job and he was glad to help. All the careful plans I constructed were back on track.

He escorted me to a desk to reserve an airport hotel overnight. An eager young man said he could get me a reasonable hotel (not the same one I stayed previously, as that was expensive). Very cheap. A taxi was called to take me. As I left the young man asked – no, pleaded with me – to write to his director and say how helpful he'd been. He gave me the address and his card. I promised. I actually did it when I returned to the UK. Youth and enthusiasm again you see, I'm a sucker.

It was with more than a little trepidation that I arrived at the hotel. I had never stayed anywhere so cheap before. It looked ok. I just hoped my mother wasn't watching. There was the usually rotten water smell, but so far every hotel in India seemed to have it, with the exception of the Himalayas.

The room was a little dark, but it had a bathroom and it wasn't as bad as I'd imagined – just a little seedier-looking than my other hotels.

As I read the guide book I was now pleased I hadn't got the train in the morning from Delhi to Agra as it was host to many pickpockets. In fact it appeared that the tourists were in danger of being outnumbered by the muggers on the train, if the warnings were anything to go by. So, another little danger inadvertently avoided.

I "dined" at the hotel that night. Not the most memorable of meals but at least I wasn't hungry. I booked my hotel in Agra. It was recommended in the guide book. I could only stay two nights as there was a conference of doctors – they sure know where to pick 'em – and surprise, surprise, Jaipur was also completely booked up with the conference of doctors. It was to be hoped no-one fell seriously ill in India during this time. I think being a doctor in India is still one-up from being a lawyer, the compensation culture not having reached there yet.

As I booked further flights, it was then I was told by a clerk at Indian Airlines that I knew more about their flights than they did. I took this as the highest compliment. I'd done it by studying their printed timetable and information gathered from two other guide books which told of regional differences, plus high season extra flights.

Sure enough when they checked on the details I'd given them, they found a flight they hadn't known about. With every second that passed I realized it was being confirmed to me, India was a doddle. Just a few wits about you, an air of naivety coupled with a don't mess with me air, and a knowledge of the timetable – 24 hour clock not withstanding and even then you would be bailed out – and you could sail through. I have to admit though to a weakness for planning itineraries. I would call it relaxing – but then again I'm eccentric.

I presume I'm eccentric. At a party they were giving, I once introduced myself as Marian and Michael's eccentric friend. The woman I was speaking to said that I must be rich. Innocently like a lamb to the slaughter, I asked why, "Because if not," she replied, "you'd be daft."

The hotel in Agra, The Ashok, was big, impressive and smelly as per usual. As an extra though, on opening the wardrobe I was faced with thick green fungus and an awful damp smell. I complained and a bellboy arrived with a spray to be sprayed. No fungus was removed.

By this time I was distinctly unimpressed by this 4 star hotel – but worse was to come. When I entered the bathroom I was greeted with about 2 inches of stagnant water. Heaven knows where it came from, but I checked out within minutes. Management were apologetic, but what use was that? It was no good pretending they didn't know about it. That hotel was run by a subsidiary of the Indian Government and was recommended as the only one of theirs suitable to stay in. Apparently their reputation is not too good. It was even worse now.

I'd arranged a guide for the day in Agra but as I was now flying back to Delhi the same day, it was to be a whistle-stop tour. I would not have time to visit the deserted city. So be it.

My guide was a good-looking, educated Indian of

about 40, on the looks of the French film actor, Louis Jordan. Our driver was a Muslim man, who didn't speak English. I found this a frequent occurrence where the guide would be Hindu and multi-lingual, the driver Muslim, just speaking his own language and I have not found out if this is by choice or is a caste thing. But on all occasions the guide and the driver seemed to have an easy-going relationship with mutual respect. If I'd asked them about it I don't think I would have been answered. The Indians can be as inscrutable as the Chinese if they don't think you need to know something.

We visited the Taj Mahal first before it got too crowded. Now I could not do the Princess Diana bit where she sat on her own but I did my best. There were quite a few people around but I was told it was not too bad. I have to be honest, it felt reasonably quiet and reflective. The pun there was unintended. I sat there for quite a while contemplating the structure. I was in the shade under a tree. I could face the Taj Mahal to my right and to my left I could watch the Indian version of the Flymo as a pair of oxen were pulling a man with a lawn mower, accompanied by another man. It all seemed rather labour intensive but perhaps the second man was there to remove any dung.

The Gujaratis were on official holiday now for their Christmas and they do like to travel. I had my picture taken again with a mother and a little girl by her husband – so there we are, young pretty mum, little girl and English woman and water bottle.

Having taken the pictures I wanted, I entered the building. Although many people have said it was just a tourist trap, it is a most beautiful monument to a much loved wife. It's exquisite and no amount of description will do justice to its beauty. Inside there was a lot of what I call filigree ornamental masonry. The views were over very green gardens and parkland to the river. Some parts were perched on the edge of the river.

Green parakeets, too many to count, glided from tree to tree, quite noisily. Even though they blended well with the trees, there were so many, they were easy to spot.

After my wander round inside the various buildings, I ventured to the grounds for another shady vantage point. So very peaceful, so very beautiful.

I'd read in the papers, or I'd have been very suspicious, that entrance fees to the Taj had been increased for foreigners. Indians could still go in for 200 rupees (still 4 days wages for many), but everyone else had to pay 1500 rupees. It had just been introduced 48 hours before I got there.

As I left to be reclaimed by my guide outside the gates, I was pestered, good naturedly enough, but very persistently, by some young men. Their hair was bushy and it was reddened at the ends. I think these were lower caste but no-one was saying. They were relentless and it seemed a long way to the car and my guide was walking ahead of me. He was no help. It was very hot – yes, around midday again – and the walk took a few minutes. First they wanted 800 rupees for some "silver bracelets." I had told the guide I did not want to buy at all today. So much for what I wanted.

They were beside me on each side as I plodded, bottle in hand the few hundred yards to the car. They were so in my face that it could have been called intimidation. If this were the UK or US I would have had a case for harassment and an ASBO at least would have been issued.

I suppose it's called wearing you down but I bought one off each as it turned out just before we gained the car. If I'd known I was at the car I'd have brazened it out. The only saving grace was that I "only" paid 150 rupees to each – but still 3 days wages for an 8 minute pester. And of course, the silver was in grave doubt as my guide informed me – thanks a bunch.

When I'd reached the safety and cool of the air-conditioned car, I asked my guide why he hadn't done anything to help me. He worked for the hire company in the Ashok Hotel. I told him he should have warned me beforehand and then we'd both know. He agreed. Well that must be some comfort! He made out that it was dangerous not to let these youths conduct their business. Of course he could just be in cahoots with them, I'll never know for sure, but I have to say he didn't look comfortable near them.

We went for lunch in a restaurant where I was the only customer. It was very good and surprisingly reasonable given that the guide was getting his "free" meal in the kitchen, courtesy of Auntie Pat, – I could see him when the door opened.

Now I'd been softened up by the hoodlums of the Taj, it was time for the carpet shop visit. I protested I didn't need a carpet but it seemed I was going to see how they were designed and made. I have pictures of a one-armed man with a picture of a tiger and a tiger skin on one side of the table and he is drawing a design of the same on what appears to be thickened paper.

It is his left arm which is missing not just his hand, which is the punishment in the middle east for wrongdoers. I would think though that it could still leave him ostracized as it is the left hand for ablutions.

Further inside the honey trap you saw men making carpets. Some weaving, some working by hand and then you entered the holy of holies, the warehouse.

I was shown a runner in regal maroon they had just made to order for an Englishman. This was his coat of arms. Looking back I think this was the double bluff. I, the English woman, intelligent, worldly-wise, (I wish) was inwardly amused at the gullability of the simple Indian. The coat of arms showed a Crown and above this, woven in the carpet, Rex Rob. How stupid or ignorant could you be to believe this? The Indians must be naïve. Everyone knows it says King Rob. And that's where I think there was the double bluff. I've an odd feeling there is a clue in there as I write this with hindsight. They want you to think they're naive. All your barriers are down. What a sales ploy.

Despite all my earnest, "I do not want a carpet" I shall say due to the heat and no air-conditioning I agreed to pay £106.00 including insurance for a dark green runner with small dark red markings. I even took a picture of the assistant holding it up. And that's the last I ever saw of my carpet, or my money.

I have tried to get my money back from my credit card and the firm. After checking with my lawyers, if, when reading this book, the name of the company and picture of the receipt is included, you know I'm on safe ground. I don't forgive easily.

I have to say though and others I've spoken to since agree, Agra is the worst place in India for being ripped off and generally swindled out of every available penny you're holding. You feel it's one big con. If they didn't have the Taj Mahal . . .

Even writing about it now makes me feel all the tension I felt then.

So having fleeced me on the "silver" and the carpets, it was time for the marble factory, I was on safer ground there as it was portable – well, the piece I intended buying was.

I'll say this about my guide, he always made sure I only saw the owner. If you're going to be swindled you may as well see the top man.

I was shown how the beautiful semi-precious stones were shaped by what look like a lathe, the colours were vibrant, deep blue, copper, turquoise, red, gold. The pieces added to the carved out shape on the marble were exact, minute and paper thin. The workmanship was so exacting, so precise, I was awestruck. At least if I was to be parted from my money, I felt a real artist was at work. They all seemed very young, about 17.

In the showroom much of the translucent marble was lit from above or behind.

I only bargained a little, as I saw a beautiful piece, about 7in x 4in for £40.00. I know I paid too much for it but as I said to the owner, it seemed fair value and it was my way of giving foreign aid. He said he wished everyone felt that way. Well only now and again honey bun.

Generally it has been my thought (with the exception of taxi drivers and their hangers-on) that if I pay a bit too much it will go back into the economy one way or another.

I have to say I was never stolen from or lost any of my belongings from my suitcases in all the six weeks. The robbing went on face to face when they could see the whites of your eyes and they deemed you had a fighting chance.

My final destination on my whistle-stop tour of

Agra was a jewellery emporium.

Now this is somewhere I'm very vulnerable. I love coloured stones. The more precious the better. This part of the world is known for sapphires, emeralds and rubies, the first being my favourite.

The ring was just gorgeous, quite a few carats of sapphires were involved and I'd decided I'd pay £200. This was like an auction, once you've decided you don't move. Unfortunately I have extremely expensive taste and although there were cheaper rings the one I wanted set off at £1,500. I realised the chance of it reaching £200 were remote.

Well I got it down to £400 and there we reached an impasse. Having bought silver, a carpet, marble, the one thing I wanted I couldn't clinch. Ah well, as I reached the door the owner followed me to it and asked how much had I been willing to pay. I said that I didn't want to insult him as I realized it was a beautiful ring. He insisted, so I told him and his face fell. Alas, he could not do it for that. So we parted friends, I with my money, some honour slightly intact and my guide with no commission. See there is some justice now and again.

He deposited me at the airport in good time, my Agra adventure was over, but it appeared that I'd already entered the territory of the premier rip-off merchants of the Eastern world. Agra and Rajasthan must be where the Far Eastern rip-off merchants sent their apprentices to learn their trade. I was going to have to have more wits about me than I'd been exhibiting recently to survive. Kerala seemed a lifetime and a world away. I do hope those gentle people keep their apparent innocence.

Across Rajasthan, my main destination was to be Jaisalmer. Situated on the corner of the Thar desert, it was on the original silk route to the orient. When planning in the UK Jaisalmer had always been top of the list.

Many people think of Agra as part of Rajasthan but it is just outside of the area, though in my mind they are inextricably linked. Agra is too worldly to belong to the other India.

CHAPTER TWENTY THREE

Finally, the cheeky Indian

So leaving Agra I arrived at Delhi around 10.30pm. The number of flights I was taking was building my confidence.

My hotel, about 500 yards from the airport, was booked. I loaded up my trolley and shot through the doors into the velvet night. I negotiated with a driver (essential or they can charge what they want) and as we set off across the road, a boy, whom I presumed was with the driver, took my trolley. We arrived at the cab after about 50 yards. Being a large airport the car park was enormous and reminded one of a supermarket car park in the UK. All bays with bushes dividing them and vast. The driver placed me and the luggage in the back and I turned to tip the boy my usual 10 rupees (14p). At this point he got stroppy and demanded 50 rupees. I refused. I'd got the trolley, I'd loaded it, the driver unloaded it, all this cheeky devil had done was push it across a road or so.

As I refused, he got mad and started thumping the cab. I looked round for my driver and he'd melted into the night. So I was faced with an irate young man and the more I snarled, "No," the angrier he got.

I was determined to holdout and then the thought struck me that he could in fact, have friends nearby. He could have a knife. Was it worth holding out? Truth was, though I always made sure I had enough for tipping as I arrived, this time I knew I'd only another 20 rupees change. I began to realize the driver wasn't returning until this was over. I was stuck in a cab, windows open, no doors locked, in a desolate pitch-black car park late at night being harangued by an angry young man (John Osborne eat your heart out,] who may or may not be carrying weapons. Common sense prevailed and I gave him the other 20 rupees and told him to go away, pointing and snarling as I did so. He walked and as if by magic my driver appeared.

I think he'd been talking to another driver, but I am now, with hindsight, positive the deal is the boy gets a tip of one day's wages for 45 seconds walk and the driver stays out of it, I even wonder if the driver was threatened by the boy and his cohorts. He was one of the lower caste Indians, the ones whose hair is reddish orange on the ends of quite bushy, frizzy hair.

When people ask me about the dangers of a woman travelling alone, I say I haven't found any. That was the only time I ever felt grave mis-quiet about my situation – so far. A great sigh of relief emanated as I reached my hotel. It looked beautiful, was 4 star, near the airport and entry to the lobby was breathtaking. I hadn't expected too much, as I was only paying £30 per night for the whole room and airport hotels can name their own price usually. And it didn't even have the usual foul-water smell.

The centre of the lobby was occupied by fountains of varying heights. The ceiling went to the roof of the building. The entrance lobby was arranged in a circle all around the centre with balconies draped in greenery and I could see security guards patrolling. Rather than worrying me, this gave me a feeling of security. My room was lovely, the restaurant was fine, only me and a couple in it. Such a change from the debacle in Agra.

Another bonus point in the Centaur hotel's favour

was a free newspaper, so I took the English version of the Delhi Times.

What an eye-opener. So many articles took my eye.

One related an incident where a 3 year old boy had been thrown over a balcony and killed. It reported that the father and his friend were drunk, celebrating getting a 25 rupee commission. That's right, 25 rupees – and the parasites of India were pulling their faces at a 10 rupees tip. The father left the room and when he returned the child was dead, apparently thrown over by his friend. Despite the horror of what happened to the child, the main focus of my attention was the size of the bonus as this effects Indian life at the sharp end. From what I understand, this was half a day's wages – well it was enough of a fillip to celebrate it. Then the article stated that a day's average wage was 50 rupees. Surely not? So now I had it confirmed. Less than £1.00 per day was normal.

Another article stated that a woman in a village – not too far from Delhi – had listened to the local witch doctor and as a cure for her infertility was told to kill a village boy of 7. This she did and both she and the witch doctor were on trial. The witch doctor had promised if she did this she'd give birth.

Whereas the bonus story showed Indian life as difficult financially, the infertility story showed that despite its educational successes, its position in the world of technology, its modern, vibrant cities, in the hinterland not too far from the metropolis, superstition, ignorance and prejudice were just as they were centuries ago.

Many tales are told of young brides in the villages dying in kitchen fires, which of course are all accidents and nothing can be proved differently. The custom is for the bride to move in with her husband's family.

This may work, but if for any reason, the mother-in-law takes a dislike to the bride, for legitimate or bogus reasons, or there is a dispute over the dowry her fate could be decided. There are too many of these accidents to be accidental. The authorities admit in the paper there is a problem but they don't seem any nearer to solving it.

Some of the most interesting pages are the matrimonial ones where brides and grooms are sought. The family advertizes their offspring like a rare edition of a Ferrari. Where divorce or widowhood has occurred then it's damage limitation and the advert reads a bit like a clapped out Ford Escort.

Since astrology plays a big part in Indian life, time of birth, place etc. are requested. Sometimes they ask for a horoscope to be cast and sent with photo and educational details.

The top of the range Ferrari reads something like, Brahmin son, 27 BA MA. Oxford, Green Card for USA. IT professional requires degree educated fair skinned traditional Indian girl. Horoscope essential. STATUS essential.

Fair skinned for girls runs through all the top adverts. This is very desirable and allowing that Indian skin is just like our white skins, a variety of pigmentations – olive, pale, creamy, sandy, freckled, swarthy etc. – it seems a little unfair to penalize the others in favour of those who by chance got the fair genes.

Of course once bereavement or divorce is mentioned all bets are off. Adverts only appeal for men to find female partners. I should imagine once it happens to a woman she is damaged goods in the eyes of the community. The advert for the divorced or widowed man usually runs as before with age and qualifications but it is normally stated re: the woman he wants that "age, education, status, caste, no bar".

It does seem peculiar to us that a well-educated Indian girl would still to be required to be at home in the traditional role despite her degree – usually either IT, law, accountancy or medicine. Dipti informs me that her brother Sanjay who escorted us, thinks that Indian women who live in the UK are unfortunate. Not only do they work full time, look after the children but have to maintain the home by cooking and cleaning. The husband usually just does maintenance. He also sometimes transports the children.

In India, the woman just looks after the home and children. Although it looks like she has a raw deal – fresh cooked food every meal – (no freezers, no microwaves normally) compared to the UK Indian wives, she's doing ok.

On a lighter note, when doing the crosswords – short, concise type – in the Delhi Times I notice wryly that when the clue is "Infectious disease" they don't mean measles, rubella or mumps. It's usually either malaria, cholera or typhoid and after reading an article in my hotel room about Filhartsia (from mossie bites and when you discover you've got it, it's usually too late as it's invaded your major organs) I was quite relieved when the answer was Rabies.

There is a heavy police presence everywhere else but they seem to be lacking just where they're needed – airports, railway stations. The air of barely suppressed menace in these places can't help the tourist industry.

Generally though (touts and taxi drivers excepted) if you fight your corner – top hotels included, Indians will negotiate but I've never really got the hang of this. If I want something, I always seem to pay more than I should.

As we drove to my hotel, it was still the Diwali celebrations on the streets and the cows had been trimmed up. Their horns were painted and adorned with tinsel and if their hides were white or grey colour they were daubed with orange paint. I wondered what their thoughts were as this happened to them and they saw what the other cows looked like.

Delhi had leafy suburbs, with mansions, enormous gardens and air of prosperity like any up-market western city. Money was evident everywhere you turned. Downtown which I never reached, I believe there is serious pollution. Prosperity has its price as LA and London can testify.

A quick call to Dipti and family had reassured them I had not succumbed to white slavery and then to bed in the knowledge that by tomorrow I would be in Rajasthan.

CHAPTER TWENTY FOUR

They rang a maharajah

Entry to Jaisalmer was around 3.30 pm I knew which hotel I wanted to stay at and now I was ready for any taxi-touts, hyenas or jackals who tried to relieve me of my baggage.

I walked off the hot tarmac into a small arrivals' hall, about 25 feet deep with my hand-baggage, I went through the exit door to find my luggage and instead found myself standing in the desert, sun blazing, outside the airport. The touts and taxi drivers looked expectant. Not yet sunshines.

I shot back inside the building before it all disappeared like a mirage. The next plane was due 2 days later. There, sitting forlornly, was my luggage. I grabbed a trolley and once again emerged triumphant into the sunlight. A voice shouted, "Gorbandh Palace." I shouted, "Yes," and a tall, very good looking young man, grinning broadly, took charge. Was he a wolf in sheep's clothing? A hyena on the prowl for gullible tourists? The jury was out. After the luggage I realized seasoned and traveller could not yet be applied to me in the same sentence, despite my years of practice. Accident, happen and waiting – a possibility.

Muktesh (he of matinee-idol looks, beautiful skin) said he would look after me. I remember Red Riding Hood going along this route before being cruelly disillusioned.

We headed for the Gorbandh Palace. The lobby was awash with tourists and a huge coach was parked up. They spoke German, which meant they could be from one of three countries – either way they'd got all the rooms. They, together with all the Gujaratis on the move had colonized Jaisalmer. My silk route dream was crumbling faster than a sandstone palace. Muktesh pleaded my case with them and they said they could offer me a tent in the garden. Not having been a girl guide, too rebellious, and for obvious reasons a boy scout, tent and I had never been used in the same sentence. I regard a caravan as roughing it. A tent was something my children slept in for an adventure.

I have to admit that the tents, and the grounds were full of them, were so large that Colonel Gadaffi would have got lost in one. They seemed the size of a small bungalow. They were en-suite and I was shown round one. The smell of mosquito repellent repelled me. It was overpowering. Why did they need so much? I'd a good idea.

Since I'd been told all about the danger I would be in when travelling, this seemed to fit the bill. A canvas shelter, albeit luxurious, in the middle of an open garden seemed to be inviting trouble. Also, one could see shadows on the outside walls when people moved about. I could imagine them selling tickets – touts would charge a premium – for when I took a shower. Big white mama extravaganza. One night only.

That's right, the offer of my own Colonel Gadaffi tent was just for the night. After that I'd have to decamp. Muktesh took me back to his own HQ – a back room at a filling station. His boss was there. A frantic conversation took place. Muktesh began ringing. Everywhere full. Looking at my face he said not to worry, his mother would be glad to offer me a room.

Then they rang a Maharajah. He had a palace, the Jawahar Niwas, it had one room free, just for the night. After that, that's right, I'd have to leave town. It was reasonable and when I got there, I was given a beautiful ground floor apartment just off the lobby. It had been a Royal Guest House and hosted dignitaries such as the British Viceroys and Royalties from all over India in the Raj. The first Prime Minister Pandit Nehru and the President, Dr Rajendra Prasad had stayed as well. Its brochure says it offers a breathtaking view of the sunset and I can second that. As I arrived the Maharajah was sitting, silhouetted against the sun, taking tiffin on the terrace as it was setting over the town and the desert, casting an orange red glow over everything it touched.

Once installed I began negotiations with Muktesh for the next day's touring. He'd gone to a lot of effort, his charges for his escorted tours were ok, so as he left I gave him 200 rupees tip. Without him I'd have been stymied. To me he was worth every rupee.

As I wanted to see the desert, he'd asked if I could be up for 4.15am. I think I can manage that say I. It had to be that time if I wanted to see the sunrise over the desert. It was about 20 miles to it. He'd also arranged for me to be transferred by private taxi to Jodhpur where I could catch my next flight the following day since I couldn't stay in Jaisalmer and there were no flights until then.

I'm a bit of a control freak – I shan't find any argument with people who know me with that one – but I was amazed when I booked a flight from Jodhpur to Udaipur and was told my seat was not guaranteed and my reservation number was 27. These planes only took 66, so I needed nearly half the plane not to turn up for me to get a seat. I was assured it would be ok. It says something about how laid back I'd become because I believed them and if it didn't happen – well, who cared? Not this former control freak anyway.

My only evening in Jaisalmer I dined at my hotel. They very kindly escorted me up to the top of the palace to the roof terrace where romantic couples dined with candles and moonlight. A small orchestra sat cross-legged in one corner playing sitars and drums etc. I felt de trop. I also felt I could be eaten alive by our friend the mosquito and I couldn't see to read my book. My last food adventure by candlelight had ended in ignominy in a bathroom.

I returned to the dining room. I was the only person there. I was served but also slightly neglected because I think the manpower was concentrated on the roof-top lovers.

I returned to my room, watched a version of 'Who wants to be a Millionaire' Indian style and laughed my head off. I'm sure they'd probably do the same if they saw our version, but it was our idea as they say.

The host is called the Big B. He's Amitabh Bachchan the most successful Bollywood star and now that he's ageing, including ludicrous dark toupee and white beard, he's moved on. I recognized him in Octopussy, but I think that was probably his last big role. He has formed a Bollywood Dynasty as his son is now in films. He can do what he wants and it seems what he wanted was to host Millionaire. He does a version in English and on another channel he does one in Hindi. But when he says "Confident" his acting skills are called into question and that's when I fall about.

The programme is very popular in India and the family in Valsad always watched.

At 3.55am I was up on time and ready for 4.15am. when Muktesh arrived. Breakfast would be on my return. It didn't take long to travel to the desert and I was anxiously watching in case dawn occurred before we arrived. You see, I wasn't quite cured of my control-freakery.

I should have known better, Muktesh was a young man dedicated to perfecting his art of the tour guide. He would go places. As we arrived at a small gathering of circular huts with pointed thatched roofs, people and animals were already about. The camels were milling and a young man in a cloak approached as I got out. He was leading a camel and he got it to kneel so that I could mount. I was expecting a smelly, matted, spitting, resentful camel. Instead I got a soft, sweet smelling, well-behaved one. I think Muktesh demanded only the best. I'd hazard a guess to say that it looked newly shampooed.

I mounted my camel. Muktesh had told me not to be afraid as he would be with me. The camel got up with all its usual grace and I pitched forward but managed to stay in place, clinging on inelegantly. The nuns at my school would be so disappointed in me. As the beast found its feet Muktesh leapt up gracefully behind me. The fact that he'd done it gracefully didn't alarm me as much as the fact that he was tucked in nicely on the saddle. I mentioned that I knew he said he'd be with me but I hadn't expected that close and he asked if I minded. I replied elegantly that I didn't mind at all. But I still don't think the nuns would be pleased no matter how I said it.

As we progressed, we passed a line of quite large tents. These were provided for the tourists who wanted to say they'd spent a night in the desert under the stars. There was no sign of them yet. My first enquiry was if the tents were en-suite. Muktesh laughed and said why bother with all these sand dunes around? I made a mental note to beware where I put my feet as I dismounted. Also can you imagine if, as looked possible, around 40 people were seeking their own hole in the ground every single night as long as the season continued. The mind boggled. Muktesh could trim it up whichever way he wished but it was rudimentary to say the least – and it wouldn't do for me. I think I'll always be 4 star. What would my mother say? Probably that I wasn't brought up to scurry behind sand dunes looking for a suitable place. And on this occasion I'd agree with her.

There were a few other people out on camels. They were all Indian and were wrapped up very snugly with big woollen blankets round their shoulders. I, on the other hand had on a short sleeved shirt. – I found it just right.

As the light began to grow on the horizon I started photographing each phase. Towards the sun the land was flat, desert scrubland. Muktesh offered to take a picture of me as the sun began to show. He got 3 and along with his other talents, I'd say David Bailey has a rival. You know what they say, "He's too good for this place." I'm going to have a hard job choosing one for the book cover.

It is there at the Thar desert that India faces Pakistan. It happens again in Kashmir, but the desert is a slightly more peaceful place, although there are gun emplacements along the border and each is as suspicious of the other.

After we'd done "sun arise" Muktesh asked me did I want to canter? Like asking a gambler would he like a turn at the roulette wheel. So he smacked the rump of the camel and off I went up and down the sand dunes. I loved it. Admittedly it didn't last longer than three minutes but I had nothing to reach its rump with to encourage it and really I didn't want to tempt fate any further. I'd survived so far. Whitewater rafting, vicious monkeys and cantering camels. Quit whilst you're ahead.

As we trotted back to the encampment one of the round huts had a sign on it which had the legend "Hotel At Fattan, your home away from home." I don't think they were alluding to my home, but it must fit someone, somewhere.

I dismounted, adrenaline overworking my major organs. Life was feeling great. I then noticed my white trousers were turning red. The cloth covering the saddle was scarlet and it was the dye that was completing the transformation. I didn't care. It was a small price to pay for desert, Muktesh, camel and dawn and all before breakfast.

As I returned to my hotel, sorry Palace, for breakfast, Muktesh said because he was already booked from 9.00 am (I'd known this when we met) he would place me in the capable hands of his second in command who would call at 10.00am. My connecting taxi had been booked for mid-afternoon.

I'd found out as we'd travelled that Muktesh spent the closed season playing cricket with his friends. This did not surprise me as cricket is the second religion for most Indians. Also he worked very long hours during the season, sometimes sixteen hour days. As I said he'll go far.

The name of my second guide was Raj, a Muktesh clone. Just a bit younger, just as good looking and personable. Off we went to downtown. He pointed out where his family lived amongst the crush that was Jaisalmer. The buildings were spectacular. I'd seen the pictures before and I knew I wanted to go there. Many, many of them in desert sandstone carved like filigree lace. So exquisite.

Before we reached the town there was a Jain temple. Once again the masonry was a work of art. The external carvings in golden sandstone only hinted at the scale of the marble carvings inside.

The interior was cool and the marble and stonework was off-white/grey in colour, whether by design or age and wear I couldn't tell. There was hardly an inch of plain surface anywhere. Room after room led through each other, each one more impressive than the last. Even the pillars, with the galleries above were intricately carved.

In the visitor's gallery, ancient bank notes of past monies were displayed. Raj said these were rare. There were quite a few worshippers going in and out of the room where the different statues of their God was displayed. In one, coloured fairy lights covered the ceiling – but this could just have been because it was Diwali still.

Outside again in the bright sunshine, the pictures I took of the temple were striking, golden sandstone, carved to perfection against piercing blue sky.

Once through the town we made our way to the fortress which must mean it's seen its share of conflict, judging by the defences in place. Inside the walls, was a town like any other Indian town. Market overflowing everywhere, dogs, cows, goats, hens, the occasional donkey and a cacophony of sound from the myriad of people – some of whom dressed medievally, others modern, some, somewhere in between, plus cars, rickstas and scooters.

There is something reassuring about every town sporting the same smells, noises and pandemonium that I had begun to associate with India wherever I was, but I hadn't expected it behind the fortress walls. One picture I took was of a woman, dressed head to toe in fuchsia pink, including in total, a matching veil from her head over her face. But the best thing was the basket she was balancing on her head matched her outfit exactly.

There seemed to be a lot of tractors in town, for what purpose, I could only hazard a guess. It couldn't have anything to do with farming that's for sure, allowing how dry and barren the land was. Then again, I've been wrong before.

As we made our way up through the town with the ramparts in the background we wound our way up a steep passageway. Its width was just enough to take a 5 ton vehicle. Raj pointed out that as we went through the archway – there were 4 of them – you could not see round the immediate corner, but the people defending the town looking down could. So the enemy would go onwards and upwards not knowing they were observed or what would eventually greet them.

In the heat of the day – yes it was already midday again – we reached the top. I was escorted across the fortress's upper buildings to a view of the rest of the town. Although dusty and dingy looking, there were quite a few patches of greenery where the trees were surviving and growing against all odds. Perhaps tractors had a part to play after all.

As Raj and I chatted he said he'd shaved off his moustache to make him more attractive. For Indian girls I asked – He wasn't interested. I asked if he liked boys? He laughed and said no – just European girls.

During all the scrabbling about over the rocks, through doorways, up spiral staircases, my young escort had taken my hand in a more than friendly manner. He'd asked did I mind and I said (Why change the habits of the morning?), that I didn't. I suppose it was nice to have someone making sure I didn't trip over my own feet whilst negotiating the ancient sandstone. He was probably doing it for a bigger tip. I don't think he classed me as a European girl though. Enterprising that's what these Indians are.

We made our way back to the main town and looked at the truly awe-inspiring main buildings which were depicted on the postcards of the region. They looked like very ornate iced wedding cakes. No, that's not true, as it says on the back of one of the postcards, "The marvellous carving has no words to describe."

CHAPTER TWENTY FIVE

Wild boar feeding frenzy

We arrived back at the HQ of Muktesh's empire, the petrol station, where the private taxi was waiting to collect me. Before we'd left town, I'd been taken to a cousin of Raj's to see the painted eggs. So I dutifully bought the eggs and realized my supply of ready cash was dwindling. In fact dwindling was a bit optimistic, disappeared was more apt, which is how my hand-holding romeo ended up with a more modest tip. If he hadn't taken me to his "cousins" where he got a few rupees commission he could have had the lot. A lesson there for us all.

With a water bottle and a sandwich the driver and I set off around 2.00 pm on the road to Jodhpur where I'd made sure I had a room for the night. The driver was friendly, good English and informative. The road was fairly direct, tarmaced and only a few minor villages to slow us down. This is not called the Peacock State as a misnomer. On either side of the road, hundreds of magnificent peacocks – not many hens around, so I think they can take their pick of the best show-offs – strolled, strutted, roamed and pecked their way around the scrubland. Although the ground seemed dry and sandy, many small trees and shrubs appeared to have survived against the odds.

The driver stopped once excitedly pointing across the scrub. Eagles, he said on the railway line. I grabbed my camera and we went as quietly as possible. I could see a single track ahead of me crossing the land running parallel with the road and there, for whatever reason, sitting on the rails, were dozens of eagles, black in colour and to me resembling vultures, but as my acquaintance with vultures is restricted to Hollywood westerns I'm not a reliable source.

As we crouched, more came, some flew off, some fluttered a bit. I took my pictures, but for whatever reason, all I got was dots. It was only after I returned to the UK that I realized I had a zoom lens on my camera. Technology and I are like that! So near and yet so far – literally. Even the pictures of the peacocks show just scrubland. They were all probably a figment of my imagination.

Well, one thing which wasn't was the camels. I have pictures of an adult camel with a young one, happily munching on the trees. At another point just as we were coming in to a small town along the tarmac road, there was a family of camels heading in the same direction as though they always used this route for direct access.

As we bowled along gathering momentum beside us was a small sandstorm. It increased in size and swirled this way and that before heading off away from us. I'd been hoping it would engulf us and then I'd have more to report, but it was not to be.

We only came to one area of water. Oasis was not quite the right word for it. Here and there were reeds, the ubiquitous shrub, but more importantly all manner of bird wildlife. And then out of the distance, just like Lawrence of Arabia came a troupe of multi-coloured animals. Mainly cows and oxen, the odd goat. One behind the other they plodded along in a measured fashion. Naturally we didn't cause them any concern, after all these were Indian animals as laid back as a hippie, as they wandered off round the other side of the water to pastures new.

We arrived in Jodhpur around 5.00 pm. For some reason associating it with the Raj I'd expected a moderately sophisticated city. What I got was the usual Indian city. Hot, dusty, and in this case, with enough rubble piled up by the side of the road to rebuild the pyramids. You know how they say on these makeover programmes, "work in progress," well Jodhpur looked like it had been going on since independence. Many of the men eschewed western dress and wore white robes, reminiscent of the desert tribes.

We passed a ricksta with fewer than the normal number of children. There was a fancy mask attached to the front in recognition of Diwali and the boys waved and shouted at us. I felt duty-bound to snap them and yes, it came out ok. As we drove to my hotel, I saw some of the buildings, palaces etc. that Jodhpur was famous for but they seemed incongruous amidst the rest.

If my morning guide was disappointed with his tip, my taxi driver looked as if he couldn't believe it. By the time I hit Udaipur I would have £1.50 left, what did he think I could do? Manufacture it? I blame going to see the cousin's eggs.

My hotel, very reasonable, was nice and friendly I had dinner there in the garden and was joined by a nice couple from the UK. We were entertained by a local band who had a precocious boy, around eight (this seems to be the best age for eliciting tips from the tourists) who seemed extremely aware of the effect his kohl-lined eyes had on the punters. They were rolled and fluttered in such a suggestive way that social services would have been knocking on the door in the UK and demanding he stayed home nights or else!

The hotel and the company was nice and relaxing

but was after all just a stop over again. The next day saw me get my flight out of Jodhpur [with my reserve seat 27] and from then on I believed anything was possible.

The plane was the same one which left Agra, then to Jaipur, Jaisalmer, Jodhpur and finally Udaipur. It flew Monday, Wednesday, Friday and as we all know, I knew the exact timings and if it were likely to fly anymore during "The season." As we know the only reason I wasn't on it from Jaisalmer was because there was no room at the inn.

I got a taxi at the airport and asked the driver to drop me at the Amex agent's offices. He got out my bags, I paid him and he seemed very reasonable. He knew I was looking for a hotel and so I caught sight of him hanging around outside. The agent wasn't what I expected. He couldn't give me any money so what exactly was his expertise? He wasn't switched on to the hotels in the region and once again I knew more about them than him. I'd always wanted to stay at the Lake Palace Hotel. The one which all the pictures show appearing to hover just above the Lake, as shown in Octopussy. Now, after my experience of foul smelling 4 star hotels I just had a feeling that sitting in the water like that would provide ample opportunity and excuse for the same experience. I have to state now, I never visited it and have no reason to believe it smells, but I wasn't going to risk it.

I opted for the Trident group just over the water and although a similar price, I felt confident I'd be OK. It was a very fortuitous choice. Emerging into the daylight, my lurking taxi driver offered to take me. Fair enough, he'd not ripped me off so far. Hmmn, well that was as far as it got me. When he heard the word Trident, I think he quadrupled the rate mentally and when he dropped me 15 minutes later charged me four times the cost from the airport (around 30 minutes travel). I was furious and told him so.

It looked like he'd charged for all the hanging around he did – unbidden – whilst I was negotiating in the Amex office. I'd to go to reception to obtain money to pay him.

When the bellboy was taking my cases as I checked in, I noticed the driver lurking again. By this time, he had come to reception looking for me. He was waiting for me to book him for sightseeing the next day. I was spitting venom. I had a quick word with the reception and told them to get rid of him as I didn't want to see him again. He disappeared. Meal ticket for the month had got awkward and he'd never know why he blew it.

As soon as possible, I discovered the pool and happily splashed about relieving the tensions of travel, taxi driver and Amex agents. I had a little rest and then looked for the "Wild boar feeding frenzy" as described in the guide book. I headed off down a path looking for signs as directed by reception. Coming towards me were two young guys who looked the sort who would also be looking for the same.

My opening gambit was, "Are you looking for the wild boar feeding frenzy?" Now I have to give it to them that they didn't blink, recoil in horror or say, "Are you an English eccentric?" but little did I know they were so on my wavelength we'd still be friends five years later.

No they weren't looking for it, but where was it, and could they come with me? They turned in my direction and eventually we reached a sort of tower. On entering we met an impressively dressed elder man. He had been the Maharajah's man. He looked after the boars, peacocks and deer, three for the price of one then. Actually there was no charge. He took us upstairs into one of the rooms, on the wall was a full length portrait of the Maharajah and whichever way you went his eyes followed you. The man was very proud of his job and his old employer.

He took us out to the viewing area above a compound. Ceremoniously he got out his bowl and scattered the food. The word frenzy is descriptive but not adequate for what followed. You'd think they hadn't been fed for a month, dust flew up in great waves and the pictures I took have a beige look to them, in fact they look like I'd taken them at midnight with a bad flash.

Outside the compound, deer timidly approached, but everyone seemed to know their place, the boars kept to the side compound, the deer and peacocks daintily picked away at the front of the observation post.

Alarmingly at my side one of the young guys had pulled his t-shirt over his head, wailing, "My allergies, my allergies." His friend looked concerned and said they would have to go and "Take medicaments."

I hung around to make sure all the deer were suitably fed. Some peacocks were strutting across the top of the walls, presumably to avoid the dust, but I've seen them perched there in other places. They look like king of all they survey. After all it is the Peacock State.

Having dusted myself off, I presented myself for dinner amongst a mainly European clientele. It must have been the busiest time (8.00pm) as the Maitre d' escorted me outside the main dining room and onto a badly lit terrace, where just two other people sat. The mossies were circling. I was quite emphatic and firmly said I would sit in the dining room. He said I would have to wait, I said that I would then amazingly he found a table for me 30 seconds later. It's funny what obstinacy will do. I think the taxi driver had finally flipped me.

As I came to the end of my European meal – curry and I are not too friendly, two people were placed at the adjacent table. My friends from the afternoon frenzy. They seemed delighted to see me. Arturo, a Peruvian, was of course dark, with Latino looks and an outgoing, exuberant personality – oh and an allergy. In fact any number of them. He worked for the Peruvian Embassy in Vienna. Now call me ignorant, but I didn't know Austria had a Peruvian Embassy. It just seemed an unlikely place. If that had been a question on "Who wants to be a Millionaire", I'd have flunked it. Andreas, sometimes André or Andy was Austrian and a desk-top publisher. They were on an Indian holiday that year, having done Egypt, China, South America in previous years. Andreas was taller, medium hair with glasses and equally good looking, but in a European way. As I was to find out for sure (6 months later) they were gay and a partnership. I'm a bit naïve like that, just because two guys travel together I don't presume anything. Even if they live together as well, after all many people do that with no connotations.

We chatted on and were really interested in each other. Time flew. I'd enjoyed their company and thank goodness their English was excellent. As I reached my room I decided to book my final flight to Bombay to arrive there before my twenty-one days ran out. I was not surprised to be told my reserve number was 57. So now I needed nearly all the plane not to turn up for me to get a seat. I was already looking up rail connections just in case. Sheer torture for the control freak. I recommend this sort of venture to anyone similarly afflicted. It's a great cure.

At reception I booked a tour of Udaipur as I had only one full day there. It was an Avis desk so I knew I was paying them through the nose – but with only one day what else could I do? We set off after breakfast to the Palace. En route we stopped at the jetty where the small launches took the guests to the Lake Palace, so I could photograph both the jetty and the hotel. Lovely, as it looked, I think I made the right choice, but it did have a splendid Raj look about it from the hotel to the launches with their red awnings to keep the sun off the guests.

Of course the day was fiercely hot. We passed a large piece of green where a game of cricket amongst youngsters was in progress. No wonder we have such a tough time beating them. Where Brazilians kick a football from birth, Indians wield a cricket bat. Any piece of land bigger than a carpet is suitable.

Before Udaipur Palace my driver took me to a park. It was large with many visitors, mainly Gujaratis (the neighbouring state) and it felt slightly cooler due to the amount of shade offered by the trees and the amount of water in the grounds. Life-sized stone elephants surrounded a pond filled with water lilies, bougainvillea climbed walls and trees, in the centre of some pools were small, shaded summer houses. The grounds had been created to give as much shade as possible, making me think that the Maharajahs and their families may have used the gardens during the hot summers. Once again my picture was taken by many families. I shall be gracing the mantelpieces or similar of many and being described as their rich, English friend. I wonder what name they'll give me.

To have white friends impresses the neighbours.

On leaving the gardens I noticed my driver had taken off his turban. His uniform was a white tunic, gold buttons and trimmings on the tunic and turban of red, gold and dark green. Apparently he didn't think I was either worthy of the uniform or he'd presumed I'd not say anything because I was a softie. He didn't know about the taxi driver then? Word hadn't got around.

On postcards the Palace is enormous. The usual off-white. Taken from above, it seemed to spread over most of the city. My driver dropped me off with my water bottle and went to join his friends, fellow drivers in their uniforms. He wasn't a particularly pleasant person. Middle-aged, grey hair, clipped moustache and an attitude. Still I'd only to know him for approximately two hours. I'd manage.

The Palace was of course beautiful. It was also very large, tiring and crowded. Perhaps I'd seen one too many palaces but I was feeling jaded and tired. I did all the major bits but it seems I exited too soon for my driver who was none too pleased when I eventually found him. 10 minutes of searching in the midday sun – yes that again – is not my idea of a holiday or an expensive tour either. As I was also none too pleased, that made two of us. I mentioned I was a travel writer studying the tourist and social scene in India and the transformation was amazing. I'll have to try that more often, say with some of those snotty devils you can meet here and there. So I'd quickly established who was paying for the trip and we went off elsewhere, the natural rhythm had returned. You drive, I look. I then made notes all the way round (back of an envelope of course). The only thing missing was my tape recorder which I usually muttered into at intervals. I'd decided the recorder should now go everywhere with me since I can't remember half the things which have impressed me.

Whilst I was away, the UK was suffering terrible floodings at home. In India, in October only two months after the monsoons finished, it was parched and dry where water should be and they would have to wait until July for the next rains. All around the sites that morning there were all these white-skinned women (all ages, all nationalities), clutching their litre of mineral water – no designer stuff here, just the bigger the better. So it was camera in one hand, mineral water in the other, a pair of comfy sandals and you were off.

We visited the craft and arts centre where dancers were balancing each other on their shoulders. Children (Gujarati again) rode on elephants and camels and artisans were working away at different skills. Folk dancing took centre stage after the balancing act. For the Indians, it was a bit like visiting Blackpool. The only thing missing was the kiss-me-quick hats. There were horse and camel rides and whole families were climbing on all together to have their pictures taken.

When I'd seen enough, my driver was waiting and it was off to a "Proper country village." Once again I saw women, head to toe covered in veils and sari balancing a basket on their heads and am now coming to the conclusion the veils have a top which holds the basket. I can see that, but why cover the face?

The village was made up of the usual shacks and lean-tos. Only the odd house. A little boy about 8 wandering around the village could easily have been Barry before he and his family left for the UK. By the side of the road an old man was expertly skinning a dead cow.

I had to presume the cow died naturally as it is sacred in India. I was surprised at this happening but I should think the only alternative was to let it rot and waste a marketable product.

The native women in Rajasthan were very colour-fully dressed but they had a poor look which extreme hardship usually brings about. It was probably the harsh life. At least, in other parts of the country they aren't as short of water as appeared to be the case there. I think the women of Gujarat are the most attractive. No-one is really overweight. They have handsome fea-tures and even when dirt poor all their saris match. You never see anyone with an ill-matched outfit.

The village was growing sugar cane if the driver was to be believed. Of course, the women were harvesting, usually after they'd taken their pots down for water. Never move there, feminism hasn't arrived. The lower caste women who work on the roads with their chil-dren only get 2 bricks along the route to protect them from traffic. They can be working by the central reser-vation and cars and HGVs are hurtling past them, but it's still two bricks, angled to make a chevron. The men get 5 bricks. So safety of men is 150% more important than women and children. What's the dif-ference between a man and a woman in India? Altogether now, – – – – – – 3 bricks.

Coming to Udaipur city again we passed a very impressive detached white villa on a hill with splendid views. The gates were closed to its drive but chained to them were an enormous Alsatian and Doberman. Until now I'd only seen the mongrel type of identical dogs in India. So whoever owned the house was either a big Nabob, security conscious, or had a lot to steal. He could be all three.

It was about 34 degrees but not humid, so it was bearable. When I people watch though, I make sure I'm sitting or standing in the shade. Self-preservation tip. No 360.

I'd been out for about four hours and felt I deserved a bit of R and R by the pool. Arturo and Andreas were there and I realized I'd probably seen them the day before when I'd had my swim. They seemed quite pleased to see me and as the pool was the same depth everywhere, my confidence was high. I mucked about, we swam about, bit of a chat, bit of a swim. Just right.

I told them I was booked on the sunset cruise. They were interested. What was that? Had they not been reading their guide books? Actually this was advertized in the lobby on a free-standing board and it had sounded just me. On making enquiries about the sunset cruise – the receptionist said, "Do you mean the boat trip?" I replied that I meant the cruise – It might be a boat trip to them but if I'd to pay and was going off at sunset on an extremely romantic lake, it was a cruise. And anyway they were the ones who called it a cruise first on their advertizing board.

The boys, as I still call them to this day – they were 35 and 31 – took details and said they'd enquire.

I duly presented myself at 5.45pm at reception. The lobby was seething with people. I asked another receptionist if they were all on the cruise, she said, "Do you mean the boat trip." How many times? It's a cruise.

The answer – the seething masses were a coach trip and only two people were going on the "Trip" – that's a compromise. I wondered who the other mug was and suddenly the boys appeared, freshly laundered and eager for the cruise.

A car ran us down to the jetty and there we were met by a smart launch, with a red awning overhead, open sides and a driver wearing the same hotel uniform as the driver this morning – but this one was a much user–friendlier person. Younger with a big grin and very obliging.

We set sail, well we cruised along, the light was still good and we were soon out towards the Lake Palace Hotel. We circled it, it looked wonderful but I'm still sure I chose the correct hotel. Further along the lake we came to the Palace used in the Octopussy film. We snapped it just as the light was fading. As we turned the sun dropped quickly burnishing the water and surrounding greenery as it went and but for the evening insects, the odd bird call, it was very quiet. The insects were just getting warmed up. This was a cruise, a 50 minute one, but nevertheless a cruise. I had two charming, fun companions and a friendly driver, what more could I ask?

When we finally reached shore again, as we alighted we were all taking pictures of each other. The driver offered to help and that's how I got the picture of all three of us under an enormous tree trunk. When they returned to Austria, the boys ran it off on the computer and sent it to me. We then arranged to meet for dinner at 8.00 pm. As we booked the receptionist thought we were all in the same room. Talk about toy boys anonymous. Little did I know it but I was fast becoming the Shirley Bassey of the trio.

At dinner it emerged we were all booked on the same flight to Bombay the next day. Well some of us were booked and one of us was just turning up on the off-chance that 56 others didn't. The boys thanked me for my company and asked did I want to share a taxi next morning. By this time we'd decided fate was throwing us together, so rather than fight it we arranged to meet for breakfast.

I had arrangements for Sanjay to meet me off the flight hoping I wasn't on the train. He wanted me to go again with him to the consulate to arrange a UK Visa for him. This had been postponed from when I just arrived.

Well, I have to admit I was surprised, I . . . . . . got on the flight. How? Why? Who? didn't turn up. I'll tell you what, it makes you feel you can do anything. Spiderman has nothing on me.

Oh yes, and whilst in Udaipur, the boys had been trying to matchmake me with the Maharaja (Udaipur Rajah). I told them I'd seen Indian sanitary arrangements and I wasn't playing.

I sent a card to chemist friends asking them could I have a special deal as I'd 30 rolls of film for developing. Said I'd whitewater rafted in the Himalayas, ridden a camel under the stars in the desert, seen the sun rise from the top of a desert sand dune. In fact, I was a walking cliché.

CHAPTER TWENTY SIX

Control freak? Not any more

As reserve seat 57, I arrived confidently at Udaipur Airport, having told the boys I might have to make alternative arrangements. After all knowing they were guaranteed a booking was as good as saying I was reserve 59. Only 7 extra people could turn up for the flight if I were to catch it.

Well, miracle upon miracle, as I checked in, I was given a seat number and not the bum's rush as I had half expected. I was on. On arrival in Bombay, Sanjay was there as I collected my luggage from the whirligig. I introduced him to the boys. We all shared a taxi downtown. This was the boys' first time in Bombay and I think the traffic suitably impressed them.

It transpired that Sanjay had found out that we were too late for the consulate and we'd have to go the next day. So we had to find somewhere to stay. As we dropped the guys off at the Ambassador Hotel, it was central and seemed ok so we decided to stay there as well. I booked a twin room for Sanjay and myself – there was no way I was going to end up with a similar bill as I had last time in Bombay. Like a good mother, I asked had Sanjay rung home to say we'd be a day later. He said in his solemn way, "Yes." I was happy, we could all enjoy the rest of the day.

As I was unpacking one or two items for the next 24 hours I heard voices the other side of the connecting door. It was Andreas and Arturo. I knocked on the door just to let them know we were there and could hear them, then found later they'd changed their room as they had a noisy air-conditioning unit, haven't we all! – and it confirmed my suspicions that they just might be gay.

Once we'd had a rest, Sanjay embarked on another round as sightseeing guide. He took us to a temple at the top of a hill. It was very crowded, teeming in fact. We approached and on reaching the entrance took off our shoes as was the custom. A young guy took them off us and put them together amongst hundreds of others. At this point I wasn't worried that I'd never see them again.

On the way up we'd bought offerings, flowers and fruit and we made our way in with them. Men at the temple took the offerings from everyone carefully arranging them. Other men took previous offerings, probably only about 10 minutes old, and moved them to the back or off depending on how much room there was. An orange streak was put on my forehead in return for the offering.

We made our way round the temple amongst the crowds and eventually emerged into frighteningly bright sunshine. We turned to retrieve our shoes, the young man never even looked up, just at our feet and our shoes were placed before us. We gave the usual tip. So this guy must have been an expert foot reader, so well did he know his job; he'd also be good at pelmonism – the card game where you have to remember the location of certain cards – as he never even searched for the shoes, just went unerringly towards them.

There were quite a few beggars as this was a temple and they were guaranteed alms. As usual I gave Sanjay my money and he sorted it out. We stopped at a pavement stall and bought freshly squeezed juices and more bottled water. Bombay seemed hotter than most places.

We next arrived at the Haji Ali temple we'd passed before with Dipti. It was a white building reached by a white causeway as it was just offshore. It looked beautiful – but what I wasn't prepared for were the number of beggars.

It started as we left the pavement and the causeway rose and wound its way round to the temple. Both sides. A small town of beggars took up every inch. It looked as though whole families lived there, but most were individuals and often were maimed in some way. Quite a few were old. I decided to donate on the way down as climbing the slight incline in the humidity needed all my concentration. The same traditions were conducted at the temple, which, in keeping with all the others I'd seen, was ornate and grandiose. Outside we could stand and look at the view with a slight breeze to cool us. We then sat for a few minutes rest and started back down. This was to prove quite an ordeal – but let's face it – not the same ordeal as if you were a beggar there everyday and this was your life as the cards had been dealt.

Of course this is what a lot of Westerners fear when they come to India or a similar country – How to cope with the abject poverty or general deprivation when you can hardly make any difference and you will be returning to your own comfortable lifestyle eventually.

There isn't an answer to this, but if you just give where you can – even a few pence does make life a bit easier for the very poor.

So back to the causeway and with a heavy heart the beggars. At the start, on the left, as you descended, sat a little girl, about 9 or 10, her little sister sat by her side in her apprenticeship years and in front of them were piles of coins. The idea was that you gave 100 rupees note and she gave you 90 rupees in change. So she got 10% without begging. Which makes you wonder why her mother was combing the seashore behind her for driftwood, presumably for firewood. I suppose any money you didn't have to spend was more in the pot for other things. So we now know that little girl was earning her family one fifth of a factory worker's wages every time somebody changed 100 rupees. I think they were onto a good thing.

I started off by telling Sanjay to give 5 rupees to all. I soon realized that I was going to run out of money long before I got to the end. It quickly went to 1 rupee which Sanjay had always said was ample, but I still gave 5 to the amputees. There was one elderly man, he smiled, life seemed good and he was faster on the move than I was, in fact faster than any of us. He'd got a skateboard but he had no legs and he shot up and down the causeway at will. He used his hands to propel himself and the muscles on his forearms stood out. As I say, his personality was sunny and he didn't look like he envied anyone. I'd like to think I tackle my small problems – in relation to his – similarly, but I'm not too sure.

Although there were more 10% commission girls farther down the causeway, I am ashamed to say for the first time, even at 1 rupee, I had not enough money for all the beggars. I hadn't realised how many there were on both sides. Sanjay had taken one side and I'd taken the other. The worst bit was I was only short by about 12 people. I couldn't look at them, but allowing they were at the start, I hope they got more normally.

We'd arranged an air-conditioned car and for that I was grateful. I sank back and let the cold air envelop me. The boys said they wanted to see the ghats. Not the mountain ranges in central India but the washing ghats. Sanjay duly obliged. We stood on the road looking over a wall atop an enormous open air laundry. There were lines of washing as far as the eye could see. If you watched for long enough you saw where they started the process. Rectangle baths about 6 ft by 8 ft steamed away. Many had a blue colour to them as though a pale dolly blue had been introduced at some stage.

It looked to be mainly sheets but some lines had clothing on them. Once the coloured bath had finished they were transferred to further baths until they finally hit the clothes line. One thing was for certain it was extremely hard work, but the whiteness of the sheets gave testament to the adequacy of the process but we all thought chemicals had to be used. We ambled back to the hotel. Walking in that heat was an ordeal – working would have been an impossibility.

After another well-earned rest we arranged to meet for dinner in the revolving Chinese restaurant at our hotel. When we booked it, we jocularly enquired if the hotel sent their sheets to the ghats and were told quite frostily, "Certainly not". Well I have to say, the Ambassador must be the only hotel in Bombay not to use this facility.

The hotel was quite expensive and rather dingy. This was the worst bathroom I'd been in. All chipped and discoloured, both bath and wash basin. Damp and white mould on the walls near the window. The boys first room was just as bad. Many things were in need of repair and I mentioned this to reception only to be greeted by an icy smile. The facilities may not be up to scratch but the staff have certainly been trained to overcome the minor nuisance of customer dissatisfaction. Perhaps it's a Bombay thing.

Although I'd had the day to spare in Bombay, I decided not to contact Krishnan and his girlfriend (the Hindu film star and singer) and spent the day instead with the boys and Sanjay. We were all enjoying one another's company and Sanjay was declared "Simpatico". To this day the boys still ask after him.

The dinner at the restaurant was expensive and we all decided to treat Sanjay for being our guide that day. I know we did revolve as the view when we left was different to the one when we arrived, but if you watched you couldn't really notice the movement. Still the view over part of the city and the coastline was great.

Andreas asked Sanjay if it were true that Indians shake their heads for yes and nod their heads for no. I wasn't aware of this but it turned out to be true. Confusing or what?

Arturo told a story of how in Delhi a beggar asked for 500 rupees. Perhaps he intended retiring early. He didn't get a thing.

We said goodbye that night and the boys and I exchanged details with lots of hugs and kisses as though we were meant to be close friends. In common with the rest of this trip we happened to see each other at breakfast. Goodbyes were said again. I packed most of my things and went down to pay. As the lift arrived at my floor there was Andreas – coming to say a final goodbye. Returning to reception there was Arturo. More emotional goodbyes and this time for at least 6 months. They were going to Goa and had asked would I go too. The way things were looking there was just a chance . . .

Sanjay and I were going on the late afternoon train to Valsad. I queried when we were going to the Consulate. Sanjay said he'd leave it till next time. The little devil. I think he just wanted an away day to Bombay.

So after 4½ hours on the Bombay – Valsad train we chugged into town. A ricksta took us home. Everyone was relieved to see us. I thought it was just because I was back from my dangerous adventures but there was a more underlying reason. Sanjay, saintly Sanjay, had either misunderstood me, or, heaven forbid, lied to me when I had asked him had he rung home. I wondered if he'd done his head nodding to fool me but I distinctly remember his solemn, 'yes'. I found out from Dipti about an hour later that when we didn't appear on the train the day before, frantic phone calls had been made to relatives, friends and vague acquaintances all over Bombay to see if we were staying there. They were very worried. Needless to say, I had words with Sanjay and he had the grace to look a little sheepish, but he still had his placid air of little boy lost, not understanding what is going on in this big world. As the youngest child and only son, I should think it's worked for years, so why change the habit etc . . .

CHAPTER TWENTY SEVEN

Copperplate at four

Once back in my old room in Valsad, it seemed like I'd never been away. Barry had celebrated his 40th at Diwali and I'd missed the party – too busy reacquainting my senses with my Diwali chicken – and Dipti had decided India was too hot for her. There was talk to make arrangements to visit the lady with the peacock in her flat – that old chestnut, I'll believe it when I see it – and talk about how little time before we'd to set off for the airport. The family would need a minimum of 8 hours on the road. I, by virtue of my vow never to travel the road to Hell again, was, once again, on the train. Dipti decided to join me. As we would be arriving early, we would visit another uncle in Bombay.

Whilst I was away, more relatives had arrived to visit, Dipti's uncle with wife and son from Oldham. They were there to look for a suitable wife for their son. He was 23 and had just got his degree. His mother felt that he needed a girl with traditional values and those in the UK were too Westernised. He seemed to agree. They questioned me closely about how I'd gone on "out there" in the big unknown that is India.

They said they hadn't to go out without an escort. I said fiddle-de-dee. It was safe. They looked dubious. I then proceeded to take one or two of my films to be developed on my own amongst much tut-tutting and clucking. I then again explained to everyone that I'd travelled India and made it back in one piece. I could manage this. So off I went. On entering the shop, this

Indian woman, around 55, said to me in a broad Leeds accent, "Do you want your films developed love?" Taken aback I agreed and we chatted. She'd returned to India and her sons after living in the UK for many years. She didn't know if she'd go back but I do know that Indians who buy their own house in the UK and then sell it when the market is good, could come back to India and be worth a fortune. Perhaps she was one of those. Could be she picked up Yorkshire business acumen, teamed it with Indian know how and made a serious financial killing. I would imagine Indian Yorkshire savvy is unbeatable.

Dipti's cousin explained to me why he only ate vegetarian in India. He'd seen the slaughter houses and the hygiene conditions he said were appalling and enough to put you off eating meat on the entire continent.

We all went out for a celebratory meal as we arrived back and this would be our last proper night together. There were about fifteen of us. Mum was treating us and even the baby went. We dined in a very busy restaurant in the open air and it was there that the cousin told me his meat theory and his Indian wife philosophy.

He said that he was looking for a bride who understood Indian ways. Often Hindus do not arrange marriages. Suggestions may be made, but if either the boy or girl aren't keen, it doesn't happen. In this case he wasn't keen. I asked him about the girl but he said all the girls were eager as they wanted to go to the UK. He had a degree, a good job, he was very desirable. I've talked to other young British Indian men and they certainly know their worth as potential husbands. They've all told me they can take their pick.

He didn't find anyone on this visit but returned 6

months later alone and finally found "the one". He is now married and has bought a house in a suburb near me in Preston. Dipti says she is very nice and fits in very well. He was a nice lad so I'm pleased he's settled.

As the evening progressed everyone was asking what I'd done, where I'd been etc. Mouths were agape as I described some of the things and places. Did they think I was making it up as I went along and had just been holed up in an hotel ten miles up the road? The Aunt and Uncle looked incredulous, and their son said I was very brave. I was beginning to feel intrepid as I basked in the admiring glow. I wasn't exactly Freya Stark, but they thought I was.

It was an early night and the next morning, just to prove my independence, I stepped out again alone. As I reached the main road a procession appeared. At the centre was a young man, garlanded with tinsel, a band and people cheering. The men were at the front, the women and children followed behind. The solitary cow made its way alongside the gutter ignoring them. I watched and took photos, then made my routine visit to Happiness and my fresh pomegranate drink and reported back at the apartment what I'd seen. It appeared it was a wedding and this was the groom being feted before the event.

That afternoon Mum and I went into town. I wanted to buy gold at the gold shop. The one where not only had they a security guard on the door – after all Happiness Ice Cream parlour had one – the door itself was locked and at least another one patrolled inside.

It was quite crowded as gold in the Indian subcontinent is used not only for dowries but general expressions of love and to prove commitment and wealth. I chose a bracelet as a present and reward for my daughter for looking after my business whilst I'd been away, and left fairly satisfied with the bargain. I later learned I'd got it for under half the UK price.

Mum wanted some groceries so we visited a shop where there were huge sacks of all sorts of food goods. In the rice sacks I could see insects moving, tiny insects, presumably starch mites, but moving all the same. I should think that the theory is that once cooked they aren't moving and are just another form of starch. I'm quite sure they'd do you no harm. Allowing for the heat and the open circumstances they're kept in, it would be impossible for any of the bags to be infestation free.

Our last stop was on the street at a stall where a young man peeled a pineapple and then cut it into a star shape whole for us to take away. It was dripping with juice and cost 15 rupees, i.e. 21p. I later ate some at home and I had no tummy problems after. Getting fruit or similar from street traders is one of the things you are warned about which will help you on your way to Delhi belly. It was at this stage that Barry said he thought the water in Valsad was treated. Now he tells me, after all that messing about rinsing my tooth-brush with bottled water etc. But I have to say that in the UK Barry's whole family only drink bottled water. So they know something we don't?

For our final night there was an air of festivity. People were coming from all over to say goodbye to Dipti. Hemman and his wife arrived. Presents were given and they'd even got something for me. One of Dipti's friends, a boy from school came from his town many miles away. The neighbours next door came in with presents and I got a silver keepsake coin. We all had our photos taken together and once again I had returned to the shiny, wet blob in the corner, water bottle in hand. Tales of my derring-do were being related and I don't think those hearing them could associate them with the rather overheated-looking individual sitting under the fan (No. 6) clutching her water bottle with her Evian spray in the other hand. Surely this woman would melt at the first hurdle?

As usual all the children were up until they dropped asleep or we all went to bed. At 11.45pm Dani who had just had her 5th birthday last week was sitting cross-legged in the kitchen doing her homework – she was at an English-medium school – Dipti showed me her work. She had written, in an adult hand the numbers 1–100. Beside them in full writing script – in fact immaculate writing – she was putting the words. She was up to forty four as I looked and she continued faultlessly through to one hundred. Remember this child was still four seven days earlier. Most adults cannot write as uniformly (including me) as she had. It was copperplate. Also this was not the end of her talents. She could read almost anything. Her baby sister who is now nearly 5 is apparently even cleverer. And to think their educational system came from us and now ours is 3rd World and if their children get to compete at world level we won't get a look in. In India, children sit at desks, face a blackboard, learn by rote, have discipline, parents support the teachers, and uniforms, which cost the earth, are purchased. Education to them is the way out of their background. Whenever you see a line of schoolchildren outside school, not only in India but other 3rd World countries, they are immaculate, well-behaved and a credit to the community. It is one of the most pleasing sights to see and the last I heard no Indian parent had to cajole their child to do their homework. They are keen and eager, even at five, as if they know their future depended on it.

We started out early for the train, our flight was late evening. Everyone else was in the minibus, including my luggage . . . Dipti and I in isolated splendour on a 1st Class train. She said she'd felt the heat this time; the monsoon rains were not enough and so it was still too hot. I shall have to take her word for it.

As we travelled we chatted and I asked as many questions as I could re: various things which had puzzled me or made me curious. Although Dipti married in her mid-20s after her education, most Indian girls marry about 18. Only married women can wear black beads decorated with gold. Also sex education appeared to be non-existent. One of her friends had a boy who liked her and when they went to dances, from which fathers usually collected their daughters, he was always making eyes at her. This was not forbidden, but that's as far as it goes. No touchy-feely. Well one day, this boy grabbed the girl at the end of the dance before the father had arrived and kissed her. She was panic struck. She would be pregnant. How could she tell her family? She kept this secret, with all the other girls knowing as they'd seen it, until someone's older, married sister told them the truth. Relief all round, family disgrace avoided, father did not need to know. Life went on.

I noticed in every backwood town I visited that e-mail shacks and long distance phone call booths were everywhere – all, of course boasting the cheapest rates. As we all know to our cost – the burgeoning call-centre exodus to Bangalore and Delhi – India has embraced the new technology with a vengeance. Even the poorest seem to have mobile phones. Everyone you meet has an e-mail address. Compared to India the UK looks like a backward cousin – or is that just me?

We took a taxi – the luxury of no luggage – to her uncle's. A nice, leafy address in one of the suburbs. The house had one main room where air-conditioning kept it icy-cold. This was because Dipti's uncle had a heart condition, he only looked about 45, and too much heat was not good for him. Sad to say he died about three years later. Of course, I sat in that room with him. Their hospitality was as always perfect. Drinks were proffered and the coffee table groaned with nibbles – one of which was Bombay mix. Now we British may think it's like chicken tikka masala which was invented for us – but in this case, I found it on every coffee table I visited, so I presume it originated there.

Around 8.00pm phone calls were exchanged and we went off to meet up with the others at the airport. They all looked remarkably relaxed given the route by which they'd arrived. Then Barry said they'd seen some serious accidents with quite a few people dead. Now this shocked me as I thought the Indian people, plus the myriad of animals on their roads led a charmed life. Nothing could touch them. Barry said the accidents were particularly nasty and had held them up twice. Given that most parts are two lanes, I wasn't surprised.

By now Dipti, her mother, father and Sanjay were very emotional, knowing they probably wouldn't meet for another five years. I kept well away. I was an unnecessary complication. Eventually they parted and we set off for passport control. Passing through all the various bureaucratic red tape we could still see the family through the windows. We all waved again and the long goodbye was over.

I reached England a different person. I felt 20 years younger, looked at least 10 years younger and although an upbeat person naturally, that had been magnified to astronomic proportions. I could do anything. Nothing would ever defeat me again. Life was so good, there to be enjoyed and I was determined I would do so.

There was absolutely nothing I couldn't do – well ok I wouldn't be seeing the woman with the peacock in her apartment – but other than that . . . . . .

Postscript

The family I stayed with in India, as I've already stated was quite comfortably off, so my snapshot of family life in India is subjective. I could only experience it at their and their friends' and associates' levels. As with all Indian society they tend to stay within their own caste.

The caste system is something I cannot address properly as I have no intimate, detailed knowledge of its workings. I can only state that the castes are as follows, Brahmin is the highest and is called the priestly caste, then Kshatrya, which is the ruling caste followed by the Vaishya, the merchant caste. Finally the Dalit are the outcasts of which there are currently 250 million. Just from what I gather, the system, which is much like our own class system used to be, is totally rigid.

From all we've read we all know how highly the people prize education. Other than climbing to the top of the tree, it is their number one priority. Even those without a good education are enterprising and eager to learn – and are quite happy to work all the hours necessary to achieve this.

No matter which religion they belong to, their faith dominates their whole life. Tradition and honour are important too. It reminds me very much of attitudes in the UK before the 1960s – don't lose face, what will the neighbours think, am I a good citizen? Children are respectful, old age revered, friendships honoured, loyalty paramount, family life is the centre of their universe – and it doesn't take too much money to create an exciting social life.

I was also told that if someone gets into trouble with the law or does something morally wrong in the eyes of the community this backfires on their families and friends. Whole families can find themselves ostracized through no fault of their own because of this. And it doesn't seem to blow over say like a nine day wonder. Even UK 1950s wasn't that bad.

Guide books say that arranged marriages are the norm, but as I've said earlier, at least amongst the Gujaratis, the parents who are enlightened listen to the opinions of their offspring and marriages for love or compatibility are as frequent as the arranged ones. A lot of this has to do with changing attitudes as much as advanced education. Amongst the people I associated with, degrees were commonplace in the current younger generation. I don't think Media Studies or "Soap Opera Objectives, BA" would cut much ice with the parents so most youngsters take Accountancy, Medicine, Law, IT or Business Studies. The latter I have to be honest, I think is entirely unnecessary as most Indians are born with the gene. The degree only sharpens it to supernova brilliance.

Pollution appears to be a big problem. Any industrial area has a huge pall hanging over it. I've no idea how they treat the rivers, but I would imagine casually. Nothing must be allowed to get in the way of the juggernaut that is the Indian economy. I would think trying to stop it would be like said juggernaut having brake failure. CO_2 is 50 times the WHO standard.

Fumes in Delhi are so bad – diesel is very cheap – that my Peruvian friend had to wear a mask. Eyes are badly affected of people even with no allergies. Figures reveal that almost 50% of significant levels is suspended particulate matter in Delhi alone. Asthmatics are recommended not to spend too long there as to breathe in the air is equal to 20 cigarettes daily and they've banned smoking in public places since 1997.

Judging by the number of scams notated in my Lonely Planet Guide, perhaps it was just as well I stayed in the airport environs in Delhi. There is talk of bogus policemen telling wild stories of riots to keep the honest traveller from their chosen hotel. Commission is generated for the taxi driver who is generally up to his neck in the scam, in fact without him, it wouldn't get off the ground. Well, why doesn't that surprise me? No wonder London taxi drivers sometimes have an attitude problem. They suddenly seem infinitely superior, even if now and again they take the longer route.

Death rituals are keenly followed, as Hindus believe that as one person dies, the soul passes into another body. As explained in my previous book about Bali, "Down Under, Roundabout and Up There", the eldest son performs the last rite at the cremation ceremony and this bit is new, he thereby is guaranteeing his parent's release from this life. If possible the ashes are scattered in the Ganges to break the reincarnation cycle.

As we know the cow is sacred. It is a Mother Earth figure – and I thought that was me – and when passing one of them meandering along, Hindus touch the forehead and pray as they go by as a sign of respect and devotion. I never saw that happen, but that's what a good guide book says. In Valsad the cows favourite cud-chewing spot was the central reservation running down the centre of the road, about 2ft wide. They aren't too fussy how they perch on it and you tend to find legs hanging off or heads sticking out into the fast lane. They look supremely unperturbed.

For one reason or another many of us know quite a bit about the Muslim religion. But a popular religion in India, and 3 million adherents, is Jainism – as at Jaisalmer where the religion is the reason for the fantastic buildings. It is a very strict religion, almost puritanical. They are not allowed to wear leather or eat dairy products and smoke or drink. They believe every living creature, including insects, is sacred. They wear masks so they don't inadvertently swallow an insect and carry a broom to sweep the path in front of them so as not to kill anything.

Jainism was started in the 6th century BC by Mahavira, who was born in the same area and lived at the same time as Buddha. One could almost say a plethora of religious philosophy was in the air of the Lower Ganges region at that time. The religion allows for the rejection of objective truth which then allows for an infinite number of viewpoints on every subject. If it weren't for the four fasting days per month that sounds rather like our house on a bad day.

Although the temples on the outside as I describe are intricate and beautiful, inside is a revelation. It nearly takes your breath away. A cliché, but the reason for this is that Jainism believes that beauty is found within. The axis east-west is generally used for the temples. You could call them Indian baroque.

Christianity in India as I've said began with the disciple, St Thomas about 52AD. But there's some debate about this and some scholars believe it could have been as late as the 4th Century AD when a Syrian merchant arrived in Kerala with 400 families. The sect of the Syrian Orthodox Church survives today and the Patriarch of Baghdad is its head.

Catholicism arrived with the Portuguese and Vasco da Gama, Protestantism arrived with other Europeans, the British, Dutch and Danes. Of the 18 million Christians, 75% live in the South. One of the Catholic churches in Goa, Church of Our Lady of Divine Providence, is a replica of St Peter's Basilica in Rome. It's a pity I never visited it. If I'd known it was there in my early escaped fugitive days, I'd have gone.

Sikhism, with 16 million followers, was founded in the late fifteenth century as a reaction against the caste system and Brahmin control. Started at a time of social unrest, it was an attempt to join the best of Hinduism with the best of Islam. They believe in one God. Many sikhs are from the Punjabi region and I noticed that most large hotels like to have a Sikh doorman, as the large turban and general tall height of the men is impressive. Turbans are often exchanged as a gift, symbolic of friendship and respect.

Buddhism although started in India, now only has about 6 million adherents in India. They lead a path to enlightenment via the Four Noble Truths. Life is rooted in suffering; suffering is caused by craving for worldly goods; eliminating this craving brings relief from suffering; the way to eliminate craving is via the Noble Eight-Fold Path i.e. right understanding; right intuition; right speech; right action; right livelihood; right effort; right awareness and right concentration. At the end is Nirvana.

There are about 12 other major religions in India but the ones above are the ones I encountered on my travels. In general, India appears to be a tolerant country, as the UK once was before our borders became porous and we felt threatened. I know Hindus/Muslims/Sikhs have their differences but away from the mainstream politics, people in the towns and villages seem to accept each other.

At the tip of Southern India, Kovalam, in the 1970s was a hippy commune. I know Goa was, but they kept quiet about Kerala. It must have been an insider's secret.

According to the guide book today it has problems with beach hawkers, chaotic development and serious prices, but mainly the garbage, with the influx of visitors they don't seem to have up-graded this essential service. The guide says most of the rubbish is buried just below the surface and the implication is that they mean the sand. I hope not. It's bad enough if it's just under the soil.

Sikkim province seemed mysterious. I suppose because of the presence of the Himalayas, the soldiers and the Tibetan refugees and not least, the obtaining of a permit.

The reason no-one looks very Indian there is because since the 15th Century the Tibetans have been migrating to escape religious upheaval. That time, strangely enough, between various Buddhist orders. Now, of course, they've fled the Chinese takeover.

Sikkim Kingdom was founded and the country then included Ha Valley (Bhutan), Eastern Nepal, the Chumbi Valley (Tibet) and the Terai foothills down to the Indian plains, taking in Darjeeling and Kalimpong.

Darjeeling became the darling of the Raj when the

British persuaded the Chogyal (King) to cede the area for an annual stipend. The Tibetans objected to this but in the meantime, Darjeeling rapidly became a trade centre, making fortunes for the leading Sikkim lamas and merchants.

In 1849, a botanist and a high ranking British official were arrested. They'd been exploring the Lachen regions with the permission of both the Chogyal and the British Government. It took a month to release them after threats from Britain, who then annexed the whole area and withdrew the Chogyal's stipend.

In 1861, Britain interfered in the region's affairs leading to their declaring it a protectorate. Tibet regarded the action as illegal and invaded to regain their authority. Britain repulsed it and the Chogyal's authority was further eroded.

To develop Sikkim the British encouraged immigrants from Nepal, so that much land was converted to cardamom and rice cultivation. This influx continued until the 1960s. The Chogyal stopped the immigration.

At Indian Independence, all British treaties and rights over the province passed to India. The last Chogyal, Pauden Thondup Namgyal ascended the throne in 1963. Since it was an autocracy, the people had begun to clamour for a democracy and the Indian Government were keen to be seen as a supporter. It also gave them a chance to lose the last princely rule in India.

Demonstrations by poor Nepali farmers against the rich landowning monasteries and the majority of the people pushing for government change meant the Chogyal was losing control. This resulting in his having to ask India to take charge of his country's administration. His US born wife returned home.

By 1975 a referendum gave a 97% vote for union with India. Ominously, China refused to accept Sikkim as part of India, hence the heavy Indian troop presence in that area. The state government is the most environmentally aware in India – well somebody has to be.

And here we are again in Rajasthan. Once again, referring to the guide book, it described Jaisalmer on the edge of the shared Thar desert was like something out of the Arabian nights. I can second that.

The Rajputs ruled this part of India for over 1,000 years but due to constant disagreements amongst themselves they could never deal satisfactorily with a determined aggressor. And so they became vassal states of the Mughal empire.

Their sense of honour made them fight against all the odds, but when they abandoned hope, it required that Jauhar take place. This is a most unfortunate ritual, especially for the women and children as it requires them to burn themselves to death on a funeral pyre. The men then rode out to meet the enemy and their inevitable fate.

As the Mughal empire faded, the Rajputs began to reassert their authority, through a series of quite spectacular victories. No sooner had they done that than the British hove into view. The Rajputs signed alliances with the British and they were permitted to continue as individual states. The Maharajah (or similar) ruled but had quite a few constraints imposed.

The new Rajput rulers were different from their fearless, brave forefathers. As with Rome, their downfall began with profligate living. Their indulgences and extravagances resulting in their travelling around the world with many concubines and retainers. They played polo, raced horses and occupied whole floors of the most expensive hotels. Does this remind you of anyone?

So by the early 1900's much of the wealth of the

state of Rajputana was being dissipated throughout Europe and America. On Indian Independence, the State had the worst life expectancy and rate of literacy. The rulers made an agreement to join the New India and they were allowed to keep their titles, also their properties and they were paid an annual stipend in keeping with their status.

Well, all good things etc. When Indira Gandhi abolished all their financial rights and sequestered most of their property rights in the 1970s some of the rulers survived by converting their palaces into luxury hotels. Not all of them made it as they were not up to the task of marketing themselves and managing their new "empires". In the meantime, I'm happy to say I stayed in one or two that have survived and I'm mightily pleased they did.

Bombay or Mumbai as it has been called for some years now is the financial capital of India – and doesn't it know it? As I've already said, mediocre hotels vie for the title "best of . . ." and charge London prices.

Now I've just learned something new. Bombay which to us here in the UK I think conjures up images of the Raj, silk routes and the East India Company, well it does for me – started off as seven islands inhabited by Koli fishermen. They worshipped the goddess, Mumbadevi, therefore the city today is Mumbai. The Portuguese arrived in 1534 and they called it Bom Bahia, meaning beautiful bay. Then in 1661 Charles II received the islands as part of the dowry of his Portuguese bride, Catherine of Braganza. It was almost like Pass the Parcel as he wasn't too thrilled and leased them to the East India Company for £10.00 annual rent.

They must have realized they were onto a good thing as reclamation work was soon finished and Bombay had a large protected harbour, where ships could ride out the monsoons. Commerce and ship-building grew and when the first railway line opened in 1853 trade was increased. After the Suez Canal opened 17 years later, Bombay was significant in its trade role across the Arabian Sea.

It says in the guide book that traders, entrepreneurs and merchants colonized the city. They don't have to tell me, as someone who has spent a few days in the place I can testify to that – they've never left, just increased and perfected their techniques. Now of course Bollywood brings a big injection of cash and many of the films are made at Juhu beach. That industry goes from strength to strength as Bollywood films have a cult following among many people in the UK, British Indian, White British, young and old.

My own grandfather traded with India importing from there and China to supply Lancashire's need for cotton. He and my grandmother visited India in the late 1940s and of course, as a trading partner were treated like royalty. My grandmother told me they had been asked would they stay, but she said that the harsh sun was not good for a white woman's skin. Allowing she was about 65 then, I think she was being a bit twee without knowing it. She said nothing about their sanitary arrangements being another sticking point.

One of the reasons Indians flocked to Bombay when the British took over was the promise of religious freedom and land grants. That is the reason for the rich cultural and religious mix in this vibrant city that today has reverted to its original title of Mumbai.

The British finally left India on February 28th 1948. The last British troops left through the Gateway to India, saluted by a guard of honour of Gurkhas and Sikhs with an Indian Naval band playing. The infantrymen slow-marched through the arch to embark on barges. Then right at the end from the enormous crowd on the waterfront came the strains of Auld Lang Syne. I'll bet there wasn't a dry eye on those barges.

In reviewing the various papers I was able to obtain as I travelled, the Hindustan Times trails the Bangalore IT Fair of 2000. 370 companies took part. Well we all know where that led us don't we? 300,000 visitors were expected. The chairman of the committee said he would develop India as a knowledge superpower. In one year Software exports were up 33%. By 2008, now only 3 years away, the Prime Ministerial target of an increase from $6 Billion to $87 Billion would be achieved but well before that. In the meantime, Bangalore and Stockholm could be declared twinned IT cities.

The Sunday Times of India reported that tourists were now coming to Mumbai as health tourists. Sometimes laser eye treatment, complicated dental care, even face lifts. They combine it with a visit to Goa or the Taj Mahal. Even after paying for the ticket, hotels and treatment plus the holiday it works out cheaper. They thought after the IT boom, healthcare would be the next boom area if they handled it well.

In the Goan newspaper were many articles about health and general philosophy. But a large article about the Anjuna market heads "Anjuna's Flea Market or Black Market?" There is then a description that says one of Goa's leading attractions is still in the psyche-delic 70s. Quote 'What had begun as a shame and be dammed and get-on-with-life option for western tourists' unquote, has developed into a major outlet for local traders. Apparently – and I found this – Kashmiris are the most aggressive sellers and numerically superior to only the odd saffron-clad guru.

There are Malaylee masseusses offering to pep you up with a herbal rub. Those taking up the offer have to strip naked behind a flimsy dhoti screen.

The drug-pushers are described as being like wild dogs, moving in groups of 2 or 3 just in case of a law enforcement raid, then they can run in different directions and confuse the cops. The article intimated this was highly unlikely, but they didn't want the cops skimming the cream off their business. At least that's what I understood it to mean.

Then there was a woman described as a white chick who just stepped out of her clothes (much to the excitement of the sex-starved domestic tourists it said) and put them on the block and no matter how soiled or threadbare they were, were promptly snapped up by morbid "souvenir" collectors. She then made a beeline for the sand dunes where the pushers had parked with their assorted wares. It didn't say what happened to her after that. Whether she got home all right, someone gave her some other clothes, she lived nearby or she wandered around naked for the rest of the week.

In the 1970s, the moral minority campaigned to stop all the carrying ons, but it generated so much profit, you could sell goods and services at the Flea Market and yet have nothing to do with drugs or nudity. And you made good money, so it was allowed to continue

The article states that the drug problem is no worse in Goa than in similar places around the world – and some corruption is known in all the different law enforcement agencies from the FBI, legislators, diplomatic corps and the DEA.

It thinks Holland's idea between soft and hard drugs is sensible. In the paper's view the worse thing to happen in Goa is that the death penalty was brought in to deter consumption and traffic. It doesn't appear to be working. The English in the article did not always make a grammatical sentence so I shall have to hope I have interpreted it correctly.

I come back again to the Sunday Times Matrimonial columns. One in a large, black lined box states,
"Alliance invited for handsome vegetarian teetotaller. Punjabi, Khastri, Hindu. He is an ONLY SON. 23+ 175 cms. B. Com (Hons), MBA from Reputed Institution. He is managing family's export business which has been established for 3 decades, having its own factories.
Father of High Status and Repute.
Residing in own palatial house in South Delhi.
The girl should be smart, beautiful, well educated, cultured, homely with regard to traditional values.
"HIGH STATUS BUSINESS FAMILY".
Latest photo required"
Well I bet that one got the high class families of Delhi with eligible daughters hot and bothered. You can imagine the look on the mother's face of the successful bride. Smug wouldn't be the word. I would imagine she never saw a pavement again in her life, her head would be so high. I could read the ads forever, it gives one a glimpse of the hopes and aspirations of parents across Delhi.

My last article is the concern (dated November 1st 2000) about how much Indians are being charged for illegal immigration to the UK. It comes on the heels of the dreadful case where a lorry filled with Chinese people was opened at Dover and most of them had died in the heat. Naturally this concerned the journalist and it stated that between £6-£9,000 was being charged, an increase of 15%.

He thinks the prices have increased because of the increased demand. More villagers from the Punjab, Uttar Pradesh and Bihar were being lured. The last province is known as the wildest and most violent in India. It was in that province the mother sacrificed a child to help her fertility.

They hear the success stories of others who have gone and want to follow. The syndicates then exploit them.

The Hindustan Times was told that most Indian illegal immigrant men in the UK get £100.00 per week for a 12 hour day and have to survive 10–15 to a room. Another £20.00 is charged for the rooms. Then the syndicate moves in and tries to take away the rest.

The article seems to be seeking to put off anyone willing to part with so much money . . . They warn a worse fate awaits the women who are forced into prostitution. The older ones are forced into petty crime.

The article also says that illegal immigrants dare not go to the doctors or get any medicines. Knowing as I do that they frequently do get access to medical treatment, one presumes that's the ultimate scare story. Indians are very health conscious.

Having finished with the newspapers, I wonder if you knew – I didn't until I researched this part – that the Greeks, Alexander the Great no less, invaded the Indus Valley in 326 BC only being forced to leave 9 years later? Their impact was so great that 70 years later, Greek was still spoken in North West India. Now there's a question for "Who Wants to be a Millionaire". Both in England and India.

I have few regrets about my visit to India. The main ones being that I didn't visit the regions of Tamil Nadu and the town of Pondicherry, Nr. Madras. (I wonder what the French influence has done to that part of India?), Bangalore or Mysore and its wonderful palace.

The Indian people generally are a cheerful people. I would imagine anyone who was depressed would either get over it quickly or stick out like a sore thumb.

I was told by more than one Indian that they liked the British because we were a "gentle people". So they've never seen a football hooligan I take it just after his team's defeat.

The best part of India – the whole dammed thing. The absolutely superlative parts. Ricksta racing in Bombay, whitewater rafting in the Himalayas, the incredible jeep ride up to Darjeeling, riding a camel under the desert stars, watching the sunrise atop my camel from the peak of a sand dune. The train ride between Valsad and Bombay either 1st or 2nd class, it doesn't matter. "Kachenjunga is clear" at 6.45 in the morning. The haunting voice of the exquisite young girl in the Arena at my hotel in Kerala, the houseboat along the canals, watching Indian life unfold before me with the family and finally the bike ride in all my finery – sari, bindi, jewellery, the lot. The realization of open plan loos, animals on the road in Valsad and even the Road to Hell. What an experience.

Stupendous, mind-blowing, whatever it is, it has enchanted – fascinated me, as no other place. Go to India, leave all your preconceptions behind, fall under the spell, you'll never be the same again, but most importantly, you'll never regret it. What starts so traumatically at Bombay melts into an enchanting visit to a country which is forever changing.

Pat Buckley's first book, Down Under, Roundabout and Up There relates, in letters, her travels in China, Hong Kong, Bali, just after the bombing, Australia and New Zealand, Thailand and Vietnam during nine weeks of spring 2003. Read the first chapter overleaf.

A Dishonourable
Guest Arrives

Xi'an, China
09/03/03

Dear Sue and Peter,

Welcome to China

No matter what people say I will never believe it was my fault I was standing outside Beijing Airport in the middle of winter in a silk dress with light snow falling on my head.

As I boarded at Hong Kong I took no notice of all the others in winter clothing. I thought they were just being cautious.

Even as the captain welcomed us aboard I felt no alarm, but as he informed us that the weather in Beijing was zero degrees centigrade and light snow, I felt a slight frisson. Had I been misinformed? Apparently so.

I stood at arrivals, facing my hosts, with a trolley full of mismatched cheap luggage (intentionally so), silk dress and short sleeved linen jacket.

I realised I had spectacularly dishonoured my country. I was not fit to travel. How had this come to pass?

Well, Charlotte (remember my Chinese student?) when she invited me to Beijing last December, as she and her mother were my guests, had blithely informed me that the temperature in March would be thirty degrees centigrade. 'That hot?' says I. 'Oh yes,' says Charlotte, 'it can be very hot in China.'

Charlotte is twenty three, has just got a good degree in Business Studies in a foreign language, and I trusted her. I now realise, as the Americans say, she didn't know shit from shinola.

You may, and you wouldn't be the first, wonder why I didn't look up weather conditions on the internet – who he?

Well, back to Beijing Airport. Charlotte's parents, Chen, the father, very good English and Yen, no English but simpatico, greeted me with flowers and many hugs. Yen had visited my house, had seen the sort of car I drive, and I think was very puzzled when she saw my luggage. She was expecting M&S matching at least.

There's a very good reason for this. My hotchpotch of small cases is never locked, is never stolen from and I can lift every one of them – just. You see it's not worth risking your job to rifle through a case where the owner can't afford matching, which is why Posh Spice lost her Gucci luggage – too obvious, you see.

After they'd got over the culture shock of my arrival, Chen and Yen took me to lunch, which sort of set the scene. We are always dining. I don't know how the Chinese keep so slim, they consume far more than I do, every stick thin one of them.

So this meal, which consisted of about twelve dishes, had Peking Duck, something which was a fish's stomach (a bit like tripe to look at) and all sorts of other things I didn't ask the provenance of. At some meals though you could tell it was a bird by the head or the feet. I suppose it's no different from our serving fish with the head on. I never got the opportunity to try snake, perhaps that will be an Aussie delicacy.

If it didn't get lost in the translation, we were at the restaurant where Peking Duck was invented – I think.

Once they realised Charlotte had slightly misled me about the weather, as soon as lunch was finished, we were off to the indoor market, bustling with designer copies.

Instead of heading straight for the coats, they were sidetracked by a luggage stall. Much muttering between them and pushing of a massive 'smuggle your granny' type of suitcase up and down the aisle. I assured them I was quite happy with my hotchpotch and as a redeeming feature I did have two matching Harrods hand baggage. It was a very hard sell to get them to agree to disagree that my baggage was perfect for me.

Accompanying us was Nicholas, a family friend, who was at university in Beijing.

We proceeded to a handbag stall. Apparently they had noted my handbag. It is an Eagle travel bag (Paul gave it to me before India). It is small, compact and does the job and as I found to my cost before India it needs a minimum of four days' usage before arriving in chosen country, otherwise there is panic writ large on my face as I wonder in which of the fifteen zippered compartments the tickets, passport and money are located. I know I have them, I just don't know which compartment they live in. I'd had seven days' practice this time and I wasn't about to give it up easily. The bag being proffered was big and impressive looking and in a country where honour is important it was beginning to look like this could be the most dishonourable guest to have ever graced Chinese shores.

The awkward squad had arrived. I must have been a big disappointment to them.

We arrived at the coat stall. Various duvet types were being inspected. Now as you know this is not something I'm ever to be found dead in. I managed to steer them towards one I would be willing to wear – slightly fitted, mid brown, almost ankle length, detailed cuffs, quite classic. One was found in my size. Glances were passed, much talk between them, then negotiations began on the price, which always consisted of us walking away and the first one to blink was the stallholder. Got for half original price. I later found out this was £40. Then I was told it wasn't suitable for the Great Wall. We started again, duvet coats at the ready. I had to choose a colour, knowing after the Great Wall I would never wear it again. And do you know I was right? I left it in Beijing for Grandma.

I was already overweight on the airlines, definitely couldn't take it. Now you know when I say I am overweight on the airlines, I do mean my luggage? Nothing else, you understand?

By this time, Nicholas was beginning to resemble a packhorse, but I could learn to live like this. Someone to pay for my shopping and then someone to carry it. Bliss.

On we moved relentlessly … did I want sunglasses, sneakers (Reebok), a fleece, Chinese version of furry dice? The latter I acquired, but it took three turns of the market before the stallholder blinked on this one.

Then Chen, who by now had got the hang of the dishonourable English guest, stated with no argument, 'My daughter wishes to buy you silk jacket'. Since the daughter wasn't there I had to give in gracefully and chose royal blue.

Honour satisfied, we moved to the next stall. I, who

could shop for England, had to avert my eyes and show no interest in anything.

Nicholas and I were ahead of the others and he asked, did I like cats? I gave my usual stock answer, that I prefer them to dogs. So he stated 'I get you cat'. I remember the feeling of panic as I tried to explain that I still had sixty two days to go, I had nowhere to carry it, our quarantine rules were very strict, where would I keep it? Still he insisted. Perhaps he meant a toy cat. I saw fur sticking out from one of the stalls, but on approaching saw only dogs. I turned to him and he said he must buy my cat, what pattern did I want. 'They come in patterns?' 'Yes, cats have many patterns, choose one.' Oh yes I see, up there, a kite . . . relief until I have to explain that it is too big to fit in one of my sad little cases. He is visibly disappointed.

As our visit to the market draws to a close I am curious about my 'new home'. Surprise then when Chen checks me into a four star Oriental Hotel. I should have realised as their address is Room 909 etc. Of course, it's not just a room, it's a two bedroom, two bathroom apartment. They are well off by Chinese standards, cats as well. In fact, probably well off by our standards, allowing they are living in a comfortable apartment in the main part of Beijing. In London it would be a very desirable property.

Thinking about it, this was exactly the size of the apartment in India and fourteen of us shared that some of the time.

The most amazing part was, Chen signed the credit card receipt for all my extras, gave me the vouchers for four days' breakfasts and a ticket for the Great Wall the next day, Friday. This is because Chinese hospitality demands that all their guest's needs are met by the host family. They do what they can, according to their financial circumstances.

After Charlotte arrived home from work we all went out for dinner, the usual Chinese banquet. Dozens of courses and you just whizz the table round. Much laughter, talk and bonhomie. Charlotte had only just started her new job on Monday and so couldn't take time off. This was her first job since her degree and although she wasn't enjoying it, it was a much needed job. More news later.

Love,
Pat.